# Critical Literacy

## Series in Critical Narrative
Donaldo Macedo, Series Editor
*University of Massachusetts, Boston*

*The Hegemony of English,*
Donaldo Macedo, Bessie Dendrinos,
and Panayota Gounari (2003)
*Letters from Lexington: Reflections on Propaganda,*
New Updated Edition,
Noam Chomsky (2004)
*Howard Zinn on Democratic Education,*
Howard Zinn with
Donaldo Macedo (2004)
*Pedagogy of Indignation,*
Paulo Freire (2004)
*How Children Learn: Getting Beyond the Deficit Myth,*
Terese Fayden (2005)
*The Globalization of Racism,*
edited by Donaldo Macedo
and Panayota Gounari

**Forthcoming in the Series**
*Dear Paulo: Letters from Teachers,* Sonia Nieto (2006)
*Pedagogy of Dreaming the Possible,* Paulo Friere (2006)
*Science, Truth, and Ideology,* Stanley Aronowitz (2006)

# Critical Literacy

## WHAT EVERY AMERICAN OUGHT TO KNOW

Eugene F. Provenzo, Jr.

Foreword by Michael W. Apple

Includes 5,000 names, dates, and concepts

A critical response to E. D. Hirsch, Jr.'s *Cultural Literacy: What Every American Needs to Know* and *The Schools We Need and Why We Don't Have Them*

Paradigm Publishers
Boulder • London

Copyright © 2005 Paradigm Publishers

Published in the United States by Paradigm Publishers, 3360 Mitchell Lane Suite E, Boulder, CO 80305 USA.

Paradigm Publishers is the trade name of Birkenkamp & Company, LLC,
Dean Birkenkamp, President and Publisher.

**Library of Congress Cataloging-in-Publication Data**

Provenzo, Eugene F.
  Critical literacy : what every American ought to know / Eugene F. Provenzo, Jr.
  p. cm.
Includes bibliographical references and index.
ISBN 1-59451-088-1 (hc)—ISBN 1-59451-089-X (pb)
  1. Critical pedagogy—United States.  2. Hirsch, E. D. (Eric Donald), 1928– Cultural literacy.  I. Title.
LC196.5.U6.P76 2005
370.11'5—dc22

                                                    2005012428

Printed and bound in the United States of America on acid free paper that meets the standards of the American National Standard for Permanence of Paper for Printed Library Materials.

Designed and Typeset by Eugene F. Provenzo, Jr.

09 08 07 06 05    1 2 3 4 5

For Jeanne S. Schumm,
in appreciation of her dedication as a colleague in the field
of literacy, her academic leadership, and her personal friendship.

# CONTENTS

# FOREWORD

Education has been moving in strikingly conservative directions. In *Educating the "Right" Way*, I show some of the damaging effects this movement has had.[1] Now, obviously, some parts of education necessarily require conserving. After all, the issue of what and whose knowledge should be taught as "legitimate" or "official" is also about asking and answering a set of questions about choosing certain traditions to pass on to future generations. Yet *how* we ask and answer these questions and *who* is involved in the process is crucial. Unfortunately, the answers that are given to the issue of how and who are increasingly dominated by people with impoverished ideas about educational policies and practices. Although often cleverly written, the books that currently provide these answers are deeply unsatisfactory.

Walk into any large bookstore or any bookstore that is part of a national chain, and find the education section. There's usually a mix of both serious analyses of education from various points of view and of "how to" books, advice to parents, and popular books about what's right and wrong with schools today. If you were to take the time to count the authors' names that dominate the "popular" books on the shelves, one name that would certainly be at or near the top would be E. D. Hirsch, Jr. Two of his books, *Cultural Literacy* and *The Schools We need and Why We Don't Have Them,* have been widely read and have served as rallying points for many groups even though Hirsch's arguments are weak and often are simply wrong.

But Hirsch has not stopped at (mis)characterizing what's right and wrong with schools and with the curricula that are common in them and the teaching that goes on inside them. He has become something of a cottage industry, producing book after book listing the facts that we all should know.

I think it is important to understand that a curriculum based on a list of facts and concepts that everyone should learn is a flawed project. It fundamentally misconstrues what literacy is about, decontextualizes it, and ignores the history of discussions and debates both about what literacy is for and about the differential patterns of benefits that come from institutionalizing certain definitions of literacy and not others.[2] It has all too often turned education into simply the uncritical regurgitation of unexamined knowledge. It has frequently reduced educational activity to teaching for standardized tests of random facts. It does have some measure of insight in that it recognizes that it is important for dispossessed and culturally and economically marginalized students to have an understanding of dominant knowledge so that they can "code switch" and so that they are not denied access to mobility.[3] However, and again all too often, the project of a curriculum of standardized facts has been based largely on the knowledge of dominant economic, political, and cultural groups—with an occasional "mentioning" of the culture and history of the "Other" to give the project legitimacy—thereby serving to reproduce such domination and to increase the alienation of marginalized students.[4] These effects are not fictions. They occur, and they occur with increasing frequency.[5]

Having said this, we must acknowledge that conservatives have been more than a little successful in challenging our "common sense" so that many people no longer see education as anything but teaching "the facts." This situation is exacerbated by an economic context in which millions of American citizens are (justifiably) worried about their and their children's economic futures. It is easy for these worries to move from the economy to a concern over schooling and traditional culture. Indeed, dominant groups have been very clever about shifting the blame onto the schools for unemployment, for example, from the decisions that *they* have made to move their offices and factories to places where there are low wages and no health care or pension costs or unions. Yet, it wasn't the schools that caused the unemployment; it was capital flight. It wasn't the absence of "real knowledge" in the curriculum that supposedly left people unprepared; it was economic decisions to lay off productive workers and to put families, communities, and futures in crisis.

In a time when the corporate sector is shedding workers, including many workers with significant levels of education, schools are seen as something of an insurance policy. The search for some meaning and stability in the face of all this is understandable, but has often generated a nostalgia for a "return" to a supposedly Edenic past, a longing for cultural restoration, and a feeling that if only we can have our children "master the facts" for the test, all will be well.[6]

Given these transformations in common sense, and given the fact that many parents do respond to the call for lists of core content, progressives and socially critical educators, activists, and parents need to take this desire seriously. Eugene F. Provenzo, Jr.'s book is a response to this.

This book does two important things. First, in an engaging style, it critically appraises Hirsch's reductive model of education and demonstrates how impoverished it is. Second, it recognizes that many people do in fact want a list of things that we all ought to know. Given this, it provides an alternative list, making certain that the reader also understands that such lists are always temporary, always unfinished, and always subject to critical understanding. In the process, Provenzo performs an important service for the many people who look at schools and see their dreams for the future of this nation's children increasingly limited as schools turn away from an education that is worthy of its name and toward models of curricula and teaching that might better be called "training." At the same time, although dealing with what many people now see as a necessity, Provenzo helps restore a vision of education that extends beyond "the facts." *Critical Literacy* is a book that is needed more than ever right now.

*Michael W. Apple*
John Bascom Professor of Curriculum and Instruction
and Educational Policy Studies, University of Wisconsin

---

## Notes

[1] Michael W. Apple, *Educating the "Right" Way: Markets, Standards, God, and Inequality* (New York: Routledge/Falmer, 2001).

[2] Carl Kaestle, et al. *Literacy in the United States* (New Haven: Yale University Press, 1993); Harvey Graff, *The Legacies of Literacy* (Bloomington: Indiana University Press, 1987); Harvey Graff, *The Labyrinths of Literacy* (Philadelphia: Falmer Press, 1986); and Michael W. Apple, *Official Knowledge*, 2d edition (New York: Routledge, 2000).

[3] Lisa Delpit, *Other People's Children* (New York: New Press, 1995).
[4] See Kristen Buras, "Questioning Core Assumptions," *Harvard Educational Review* 69 (Spring 1999), pp. 67–93. For a thoughtful discussion of Hirsch's views of literacy and their pedagogical and political implications, see Robert Miklitsch, "The Politics of Teaching Literature," in Henry Giroux and Kostas Myrsiades, eds., *Beyond the Corporate University* (Lanham: Rowman and Littlefield, 2001), pp. 267–285.
[5] See Linda McNeil, *The Contradictions of School Reform* (New York: Routledge, 2000); and Pauline Lipman, *High Stakes Schooling* (New York: Routledge/Falmer, 2004).
[6] Apple, *Educating the "Right" Way.*

# ACKNOWLEDGMENTS

I would like to thank the many people who have helped me in writing this book. Most important is my wife Asterie Baker Provenzo. Throughout the formulation and writing of this work she has listened to ideas and suggested items that would provide a response to Hirsch.

I would also like to thank my students and colleagues at the University of Miami who have helped me with items for this book. Particular thanks go to Manuel Bello and John P. Renaud for their careful reading of the manuscript and useful suggestions. Thanks also to Lina Chiappone, Walter Fajet, Annis Shaver, Ben Lester and Angie Toombs. My department chair, Jeanne S. Schumm, has provided a supportive environment, along with Dean Sam Yarger. Colleagues including Bill Blanton, Arlene Brett, Arlene Clachar, Gil Cuevas, Harry Forgan, Sandra Fradd, Beth Harry, Janette Klingner, and Bob Moore have taught me as educators about making theory and practice one. Alan Whitney kept the computers going. Thanks go to Eric Bredo, University of Virginia, who helped set the idea of this book in motion. A discussion with him at a meeting of the American Educational Studies Association led me to reflect more carefully about Hirsch and his work. Special thanks go to Michael W. Apple at the University of Wisconsin as well as to Karen Wolney and Catherine Bernard at Routledge/Falmer. Ken Saltman at DePaul University deserves special thanks for providing a helpful critical review. Thanks go to the editorial and marketing staff at Paradigm Publishers—particularly Dean Birkenkamp, Beth Davis, Dianne Ewing, Melanie Stafford, and Alison Sullenberger.

Finally, I would like to acknowledge Miami, Florida, with all its challenging diversity, for providing me a broader perspective on cultural literacy than I would have had if I lived and worked in a more traditional environment.

*Eugene F. Provenzo, Jr.*
Armistead Churchill Gordon House
Staunton, Virginia
June 2005

# INTRODUCTION

What knowledge is most worthy? and its corollary, What should we teach our children? are deceptively simple questions. The nineteenth century English critic Matthew Arnold had an immediate answer when he said, "the best that has been said and thought in the world."[1] When he made this argument Arnold was thinking of the Western cultural tradition.

In recent years, the question of what knowledge is most worthy has emerged as part of the contemporary debate on education and schooling. It is related to the larger question of who and what is an American? Contemporary conservative critics from William Bennett to Alan Bloom, Harold Bloom, E.D. Hirsch Jr., Chester Finn Jr., Diane Ravitch, and Arthur Schlesinger Jr. believe they have the answer. America is what its most successful and powerful people have been—their literature, history, personal stories, and traditions.

This type of answer assumes that America—perhaps more properly the United States and its culture—is a melting pot where differences of race, ethnicity, wealth, and religion are eliminated in the unifying crucible of culture. It assumes a conservative model of what it means to be an American. I believe that this model is naive and self-serving and flies in the face of the American experience.

The United States has been characterized by its diversity since its earliest history. It is a diversity that has grown and expanded along with its people. While based heavily in Anglo-Saxon traditions, its culture has been shaped not only by a wide range of European cultures but increasingly by contributions from world cultures. This diversity has been one of our great strengths and also one of our greatest challenges. For critics such as Arthur Schlesinger Jr., it has the potential to bring about "the fragmentation, resegregation, and tribalization of American life."[2] For him, and like-minded critics, the question of what we should teach our children is ultimately a much larger question about who we are as Americans, and what is the direction of our culture.

1

Like the conservative critics listed above, I also believe that the question of what we should teach our children is essential to American democracy. However, I have very different reasons for believing that it is important than do the critics listed above. I believe that if we are to have a truly just and equitable society— a truly democratic culture—then not only must power and wealth be shared, but also so must the literature, history, personal stories, and traditions of all of our people. This means not only black and white, Asian, African and European, but gay and straight, radical and conservative, religious and nonreligious. We as a people, as our founding "mothers" and "fathers" intended, need to be involved in a constant process of constructing and evolving the meaning of being an American.

If we follow Arnold's dictum of having our children learn "the best that has been said and thought in the world," then we must realize that this involves an essential process of dialogue, interaction, negotiation, and mutual understanding with all our peoples and cultures. Democracy is not a fixed noun, but an active verb, as is culture an activity and not merely a thing. It is here where I so strongly disagree with Hirsch and his followers, and why I believe that his educational and cultural model is essentially authoritarian, aristocratic, elitist, and ultimately, undemocratic.

As will be seen in the pages of this book, I object to many things about E. D. Hirsch, Jr. and his work. This work is intended as a challenge to many of his ideas about cultural literacy. I object, for example, that he has appropriated the use of the term "cultural literacy" for his own narrow ideological purposes.[3] I object to the fact that he has decided, largely by himself, what it is to be American, and who and what is un-American. I believe that true "cultural literacy" is something much more dynamic and meaningful—and ultimately democratic—than he postulates.

This book situates itself in the American "culture wars" of the late twentieth and early twenty-first centuries. It ultimately asks the questions Who is an American? and What is American? In part, this project was undertaken in response to the publication of Hirsch's *The Schools We Need and Why We Don't Have Them* (1996),[4] which uses his earlier book, *Cultural Literacy* (1987), as its foundation.[5] Were it not for the publication of *The Schools We Need*, and the renewal of the conservative educational program under the George W. Bush administration, I probably would not have written this book.

In this context, Michael Apple's ideas are extremely valuable. In *Educating the Right Way* (2001), Apple situates Hirsch's and like-minded conservatives' thinking in what the cultural critic Raymond Williams describes as "residual forms." According to him, their vision is essentially romantic and hearkens back to an earlier era where "real knowledge" was accepted unquestioningly, and people "knew their place" and did not challenge the natural order. Apple lists under the effects of this ideological position mandatory and statewide testing, a return to higher standards, a reviving of the Western tradition, patriotism, and various models of character education.[6] Underlying this movement is what he believes is "a fear of the 'Other,'" fear that "is expressed in its support for a standardized national curriculum, its attacks on bilingualism and multi-culturalism, and its insistent call for raising standards."[7]

Apple points out that "behind much of the neoconservative position is a clear sense of loss—a loss of faith of imagined communities, of a nearly pastoral vision of like-minded people who share norms and values and in which the 'Western tradition' reigned supreme."[8] Conservatives such as William Bennett, Alan Bloom, Harold Bloom, Chester Finn Jr., Diane Ravitch, Arthur Schlesinger Jr., and E. D. Hirsch, Jr. all hearken back in one way or another to this "pastoral dream," as do conservative political figures such as George W. Bush.

Many of the leaders of this movement contradict their desire for a more moral and traditional culture through their actions. William Bennett (former head of the National Endowment for the Humanities, secretary of education, and "Drug Czar"), for example, has made a cottage industry out of writing works such as *The Book of Virtues,* in which he declares that "we should know that too much of anything, even a good thing, may prove to be our undoing ... [We] need ... to set definite boundaries on our appetites."[9] This is said by a man who appears to be a degenerate gambler whose casino gambling losses have been recently reported as more than $8 million.[10]

Bennett, like his fellow conservative Chester Finn Jr., calls for a return to a simpler culture and more traditional public schools, while being actively involved in get-rich-quick schemes focused on the privatization of these schools. Bennett, for example, has been closely associated with the Edison School Project—considered by many to be the main effort to privatize public education in the United States. In 1999 he started K12, a company based in McLean, Virginia, that targets home-schoolers with online lessons based on Hirsch's Core Foundation Curriculum.[11] Likewise, Finn is one of the founding partners of the Edison Project, and has a potentially significant interest in its success as a publicly traded company.[12]

As is the case with figures such as Bennett and Finn, Hirsch has gained a wide following among conservatives and the general public. In many regards, he has perhaps the most clearly articulated philosophy of education of any of the conservative pundits in education. In addition to the publication of *Cultural Literacy* and *The Schools We Need*, Hirsch has introduced his ideas on education through his promotion of the Core Knowledge Foundation, based in Charlottesville, Virginia, which not only includes extensive curriculum materials but also supports an annual conference and a national network of schools based on his ideas about education (to be found online at coreknow@coreknowledge.org).

*Cultural Literacy*, which is the foundation of Hirsch's work in education, was widely reviewed and critiqued when it was published. Together with Alan Bloom's bestseller, *The Closing of the American Mind* (1987), it was one of the main texts of the culture wars of the late 1980s and early 1990s.[13] It is in point of fact part of a larger conservative movement in contemporary education that goes back to the 1983 publication of *A Nation at Risk* and the conservative educational "reform" of the Reagan administration.[14]

Perhaps the most interesting and certainly the most controversial aspect of Hirsch's *Cultural Literacy* is the appendix, "What Literate Americans Know." Hirsch explains that his list of 5,000 items "is provisional; it is intended to illustrate the character and range of knowledge literate Americans tend to share."[15] While Hirsch admits that there may be some disagreement over the items included in his list, since "different literate Americans have slightly different conceptions of our shared knowledge," it is clear from the main content of *Cultural Literacy* and subsequent publications of his that Hirsch considers the items included to be part of a "core" or essential system of knowledge.[16]

Hirsch's *Cultural Literacy* subsequently followed by his curriculum guides for the Core Knowledge Series (*What Your First Grader Needs to Know* (1991); *What Your Second Grader Needs to Know* (1991); *What Your Third Grader Needs to Know* (1992); *What Your Fourth Grader Needs to Know* (1992); *What Your Fifth Grader Needs to Know* (1993); *What Your Sixth Grader Needs to Know* (1993); along with *A First Dictionary of Cultural Literacy: What Our Children Need to Know* (1989); *The Dictionary of Cultural Literacy* (1993); and *The Schools We Need and Why We Don't Have Them* (1996), as well as numerous short articles and speeches, represent an ongoing political and cultural project. It is a project that is closely connected to the larger conservative movement in education and has as its purpose the increasing standardization of the curriculum—efforts seen reflected in the implementation of the "No Child Left Behind" legislation of the Bush administration. It is a project that as Michael Apple explains has as its object "changing our common sense, altering the most basic categories, the key words we employ to understand the social and educational world and our place in it."[17] It is a project that, because of its success and influence, demands a very careful critique.

That is the purpose of this book—to challenge the assumptions of E. D. Hirsch, Jr. by means of a cultural critique. In doing so, I repeat Hirsch's quote found at the beginning of *The Schools We Need* from the Roman poet Juvenal: "Who will reform the reformers?"[18] It is largely in the spirit of Juvenal's quote that I undertake this analysis of Hirsch. My question is, Who will reform Hirsch? Who will ask the questions that Hirsch does not dare to ask or know how to ask? Who will speak the words he does not speak or know how to speak? Who will reform Hirsch's followers?

Like Hirsch's books on education, this book is about the meaning of cultural literacy, and what it means to be educated in the United States. It is also about how curriculum and culture are constructed and the role and meaning of education in a democratic society. I directly challenge Hirsch's personal construction of culture and his philosophy of education. While I accept many of the ideas and traditions of the Western literary and cultural canon that both he *and I* consider important, I object to the essential arrogance of his construction of this vital tradition, his limited perspective, and his tendency to perpetuate models of patriarchy, domination, and exclusion.

This book is a primer in the essentials of *critical literacy*. It assumes that there is no such thing as neutral knowledge, and that Hirsch's model and the conservative educational agenda in education, in fact, deny not only the United States' diversity but its democratic traditions of inclusion and the reality of who and what we have been as a people. I would maintain that Hirsch and the conservatives' educational outlook provides a highly selective and limiting democratic vision—one that discourages dialogue and denies our history. In the end, I believe that it is not only undemocratic but also un-American and contradicts the American experience.

Like Hirsch's *Cultural Literacy*, this book is fraught with problems and limitations. For example, it also includes a list of 5,000 things every educated American *ought to know*. I emphasize *ought to know* rather than Hirsch's use of *need to know*. Many of the terms I have included are consciously political. They are terms that often represent different threads in the fabric of American culture and life than those drawn out by Hirsch and his fellow conservatives. Many of the terms are included with the idea of their provoking dialogue and discussion concerning who and what we are as a culture, as well as what we should become.

None of the items on this list are included by Hirsch on his list. My list excludes much that is important, while often emphasizing the personal interests and peculiarities of its author. Unlike Hirsch's list, it is not intended to represent a canon of knowledge, but instead, as emphasized above, is intended to be a starting point for dialogue, reflection, and exchange. I encourage others to add to my list, or to create totally new lists of their own.

My list of 5,000 items every educated American "ought to know" is constructed deliberately with the idea of including ideas, concepts, and people Hirsch left out of his list. It is "un-American" compared to his list, but very American in terms of whom I believe we as Americans actually are, and are becoming. I would, in fact, argue that Hirsch's list, by excluding so much, represents a type of "un-American literacy," one that denies our heritage and the reality of the American experience. My list, unlike Hirsch's, suggests many questions those in power in American culture rarely ask, or at least not in public.

These questions certainly can be found in the research literature dealing with education and cultural studies, educational philosophy, the history of education, the sociology of education, and curriculum theory—in other words what is commonly referred to as the social foundations of education. They include:

- What constitutes really useful knowledge? Whose interest does it serve? What kinds of social relations does it structure and at what price?[19]

- What and whose knowledge will be included in a national curriculum?[20]

- What is literacy? What does it mean to be literate?

- How does school knowledge enable those who have been generally excluded from schools to speak and act with dignity?[21]

- What are the basics and why are we teaching them?[22]

- Who speaks in a culture? Whose voice is heard?[23]

- How can a democracy be sustained without an ethic of criticism?[24]

I would personally add to this list, Can there be a shared meaning or commonality in what it means to be an American?

These questions are addressed in detail in the pages that follow. They represent issues largely avoided or ignored by Hirsch. Their answers represent a significant critique of Hirsch and the educational conservatives' ideas on education and what it means to be culturally literate.

\*         \*         \*

This book is divided into two parts. The first provides an overview and critique of Hirsch and his concept of "cultural literacy"—one I maintain is essentially un-American. It includes the questions asked above. Once again, the questions I have chosen reflect my own predilections and biases—just as Hirsch's reflects his predilections and biases. I am not claiming that they are the best questions that can be asked or the only questions that should be asked. They are intended as a starting point for dialogue—the beginning of a broader discussion about the meaning of culture and education. In the second part of the book I have created my own list of 5,000 cultural terms—terms and concepts that I believe are fundamental and basic for those wanting to be critically literate and engaged citizens. These are terms and concepts that every educated citizen *ought to know*.

My alternative list of cultural terms may at first seem to be just another list like Hirsch's. I believe, however, that its intention and purpose is significantly different. It is not presented as one that every educated American "needs to know." Instead it is a list educated Americans "ought to know." By using the word "ought," I emphasize a body of knowledge that is useful—that might be helpful in understanding a wide range of ideas, traditions, and people. It also suggests that these are things that ought to be known for people's own good and protection. Unlike Hirsch, I believe that I avoid a patronizing tone—one that I believe is implicit in the use of the phrase "needs to know."

My list is not intended to represent a canon. I believe that there are many other lists that could be created. I would like to think that the list's primary purpose is to challenge the canonicity of Hirsch's list and to encourage a dialogue about what educated Americans ought to know. In this context, I understand cultural literacy, like democracy, to be an active process, rather than a fixed phenomenon.

This is not meant to be a polite book. Some readers may view it as a liberal educator's attempt to engage Hirsch in a battle in the culture wars. So be it. It should be considered a *polemic*—in other words, consciously adversarial—a critical response to Hirsch and other educational conservatives. Unlike Hirsch's polemics, including *Cultural Literacy* and *The Schools We Need*, I hope I have written it with greater concern for accuracy in its scholarship and openness in its dialogue.[25]

Let there be no mistake concerning my views. I believe that the conservative agenda that has dominated American education for the past two decades—and its leaders like Hirsch—have made schools less democratic and ultimately un-American, less learning and student-oriented and ultimately less humane. I think that the political and personal ends of reformers have often been served more than the needs of our children and our society. Although our public schools need to be improved along many different lines, the solutions proposed by Hirsch and his fellow conservatives have the potential to create a far worse condition than the problems that actually exist. In fact, I would argue that many of the problems of contemporary public schooling are a result of false assumptions and failed reforms that have been part of the conservative agenda over the past twenty years.

I would further maintain that many of the problems facing our schools have to do with much larger issues at work in our society. The problems that we are seeing increasingly manifested in our schools are, I believe, symptoms of a much larger cultural and social crisis—one that is a result of the failure of the traditions of modern thought and science, of modern community and culture. It not only spiritual crisis but one that is rooted in our failure as a society to sufficiently cherish both human and natural resources—resources upon which our future depends. It is a crisis of democratic thought and action.

Ironically, Hirsch and I are concerned with many of the same issues about our culture and educational system. Our differences lie in how we have chosen to address the problem of the schools, and in my belief that Hirsch's solutions to problems may only make them worse.

I believe that there are no simple answers to the problems of the public schools. We have the obligation, however, not only to try to understand our own history, but also to direct it. As I will argue in the pages that follow, we are not powerless in responding to the crisis facing American public education.

I believe that our main limitation lies in our inability to engage in careful self-analysis and dialogue. Such self-analysis requires us to look at what we teach and why we teach it. On a local level, in our communities and in our classrooms, we must ask who benefits most from what we teach and why?

I hope that this book and its arguments will at the very least encourage a constructive dialogue—if not a passionate debate. We owe our children and American culture nothing less.

---

## Notes

[1] See Matthew Arnold, *Literature and Dogma: An Essay Towards a Better Apprehension of the Bible* (Boston: J. R. Osgood, 1874. See also *Culture and Anarchy: An Essay in Political and Social Criticism,* New York: MacMillan, 1882.

[2] Arthur M. Schlesinger Jr., *The Disuniting of America* (New York: W. W. Norton, 1991), p. 18.

[3] Hirsch did coin the phrase cultural literacy. See: C. A. Bowers, *Cultural Literacy for Freedom: An Existentialist Perspective on Teaching, Curriculum, and School Policy* (Eugene, OR: Elan, 1974).

[4] E. D. Hirsch, Jr., *The Schools We Need and Why We Don't Have Them* (New York: Doubleday, 1996).

[5] E. D. Hirsch, Jr., *Cultural Literacy: What Every American Needs to Know* (New York: Vintage Books, 1988).

[6] Michael W. Apple, *Educating the "Right Way"* (New York: Routledge Falmer, 2001), p. 46.

[7] Ibid.

[8] Ibid, p. 48.

[9] Quoted by Joshua Green, "The Bookie of Virtue," *Washington Monthly*, June 2003. Available online at: http://www.washington monthly.com/features/2003/0306.green.html.

[10] Ibid.

[11] See the K12 website at: http://www.k12.com.

[12] See Chester E. Finn Jr.'s profile at the Media Transparency website, http://www.mediatransparency.org/people/chester_finn.htm.

[13] Alan Bloom, *The Closing of the American Mind* (New York: Simon and Schuster, 1987).

[14] U.S. Department of Education, *A Nation at Risk: The Imperative of Educational Reform* (Washington, D.C.: Government Printing Office, 1983).

[15] E. D. Hirsch, Jr., *Cultural Literacy*, p. 146.

[16] Ibid. The notion that "different literate Americans have *slightly* [emphasis mine] different conceptions of our shared knowledge" is indicative of Hirsch's lack of understanding that curriculum is a contested field.

[17] Apple, *Educating the "Right Way,"* p. 9.

[18] *Satires*, 6, 1, 347.

[19] Henry Giroux, *Living Dangerously: Multiculturalism and the Politics of Difference* (New York: Peter Lang, 1993), p. 16.

[20] Kristin L. Buras, "Questioning Core Assumptions: A Critical Reading of and Response to E. D. Hirsch, Jr.'s *The Schools We Need and Why We Don't Have Them,"* *Harvard Educational Review* 69, No. 1 (Spring 1999), p. 85.

[21] Giroux, *Living Dangerously*, p. 16.

[22] Joe Kincheloe and Shirley R. Steinberg, eds., *Thirteen Questions: Reframing Education's Conversation*, 2d ed. (New York: Peter Lang, 1995), p. 13.

[23] Henry Giroux, *Border Crossings: Cultural Workers and the Politics of Education* (New York: Routledge, 1992), p. 26.

[24] Buras, *op. cit.*, p. 85.

[25] The Merriam Webster Online Dictionary defines polemic as follows: "po·lem·ic Pronunciation: po-'le-mik Function: noun Etymology: French polémique, from Middle French, from polemique controversial, from Greek polemikos warlike, hostile, from polemos war; perhaps akin to Greek pelemizein to shake, Old English ealfelo baleful Date: 1638 1 a : an aggressive attack on or refutation of the opinions or principles of another b : the art or practice of disputation or controversy —usually used in plural but sing. or plural in constr. 2: an aggressive controversialist: disputant po·lem·i·cist." See: http://www.m-w.com/dictionary.

# CULTURAL LITERACY AND THE LOSS OF DEMOCRATIC DIALOGUE

> Practical men, who believe themselves to be quite exempt from any intellectual influences, are usually the slaves of some defunct economist.
> —John Maynard Keynes as quoted by E. D. Hirsch, Jr., in *The Schools We Need and Why We Don't Have Them* (1996, p. 1)

This is a book about words. It is about words that are spoken and words that are not spoken. It is about ideas that are taught in our schools and ideas that are disregarded or discredited. It is a book that asks why certain questions are asked and why others are not. It is a book about learning and about whose knowledge is important and valued. It is a book about power: who has it and who doesn't have it. It is about whose voices are heard and why. It is about who isn't heard and why. It is a book about the purpose of education in American culture. It is a book about the meaning of cultural and critical literacy.

E. D. Hirsch, Jr., as perhaps the most prominent and successful advocate of traditional and "back-to-basics" curriculums in the United States, calls for an educational model that focuses around what he defines as "cultural literacy." According to Hirsch, cultural literacy is essential to the perpetuation of a democratic culture. It is part of "a common knowledge or collective memory." It "allows people to communicate, to work together, to live together. It forms the basis of communities, and if it is shared by enough people, it is a distinguishing characteristic of a national culture."[1]

Hirsch believes that "such a body of information is shared by literate Americans ... and that this body of information can be identified and defined."[2] For him: "Cultural literacy, unlike expert knowledge, is meant to be shared by everyone. It is that shifting body of information that our culture has found useful, and therefore worth preserving."[3] This shared knowledge, according to Hirsch, is the foundation of our public discourse. It provides the common vocabulary and ideas that make it possible for us to read a newspaper, understand our peers and leaders, and engage in political and social discourse. It is, for Hirsch, "part of what makes Americans American."[4]

As part of his effort to define the knowledge necessary to be a literate American, Hirsch includes a "preliminary" list in an appendix at the conclusion of *Cultural Literacy* of 5,000 items of "What Literate Americans Know." The list was developed in collaboration with the historian Joseph Kett and physicist James Trefil, both professors with Hirsch at the University of Virginia.

Hirsch believes that to warrant a place on his list of "5,000 essential names, phrases, dates, and concepts … an item must have lasting significance. Either it has found a place in our collective memory or it has the promise of finding such a place."[5] He warrants that determining whether or not an item is significant is often difficult and has employed the device that if a person or event has been recognized for more than fifteen years then it can be included on the list.

Hirsch and his co-authors do not take into account the extent to which this seemingly reasonable limitation is in reality very limiting. Should video game violence be excluded from the list as a cultural issue because it has only emerged as an issue since the early 1990s? Is Columbine, as a word, geographical place, and a tragic historical event, something that simply does not enter the discourse of American culture (and therefore inclusion on the "list") because it is too new? "What about September 11, 2001?" When he published *Cultural Literacy* in 1987, should the acronym AIDS (Acquired Immune Deficiency Syndrome) have been left off because it had not been "tested by time"?

Why is it that Hirsch and his co-authors fail to recognize that what they are involved in in their creation of a "core system of knowledge" is, in fact, a highly political undertaking? Take, for example, the following quote from the Preface of *Cultural Literacy*.

> Cultural literacy constitutes the only sure avenue of opportunity for disadvantaged children, the only reliable way of combating the social determinism that now condemns them to remain in the same social and educational condition as their parents.[6]

Hirsch maintains that "Literate culture is the most democratic culture in our land: it excludes nobody; it cuts across generations and social groups and classes; it is not usually one's first culture, but it should be everyone's second, existing as it does beyond the narrow spheres of family, neighborhood, and region."[7]

What proof does Hirsch have of this idea? Significant evidence from a wide range of sociologists and educational theorists suggests that education and traditional literacy tend to replicate systems of power and privilege from one generation to the next. Randall Collins, for example, argues that educational institutions—including the content of their curriculum—reinforce status groups and the value systems associated with certain professions and strata of the society.[8] In a related argument J. W. Meyer argues that specific organizational "charters" serve as "selection criteria" in the educational and occupational marketplace.[9] C. H. Persell, S. Catsambis, and P. Cookson clearly show this in the relationship between attendance at elite private schools and acceptance into elite universities. According to their findings, graduates of select private schools gain advantages for admission to highly selective colleges and universities as a result of special charters, highly developed social networks, parental wealth, preference for children of alumni, and selective coursework.[10]

Hirsch and his conservative followers do not seem to have much awareness that the type of curriculum described in *Cultural Literacy, The Schools We Need and Why We Don't Have Them,* and the Core Knowledge Curriculum in general, is not only geared toward those who already have power, but functions to reinforce existing lines of economic and social privilege. There is a remarkable lack of self-reflection and criticism in Hirsch's work. Nowhere does he ask about his assumptions, his biases, or how he constructs knowledge. Nowhere does he, or other conservatives like him, ask who benefits most from his model of cultural literacy, or from the conservative program in education.

## Hirsch as a Leader of the Conservative Movement in Contemporary Education

Those individuals reading Hirsch who are not particularly familiar with the conservative educational movement in the United States during the last twenty-five years may not realize the extent to which he and his ideas are connected to a larger social and political system. Hirsch readily acknowledges his connections. In the introduction to *Cultural Literacy*, for example, he explains how the "single greatest impetus" to write the book came from Dianne Ravitch, the conservative educational historian and a senior educational administrator during the Reagan presidency—a figure who also served as an advisor to George W. Bush in his 2000 campaign for the presidency.

Throughout his writings and speeches Hirsch acknowledges Ravitch's influence and praises other conservative educational leaders such as Chester Finn, Jr., assistant secretary for educational research in the U.S. Department of Education during the Reagan administration (a frequent co-author with Diane Ravitch), and William J. Bennett, former head of the National Endowment for the Humanities, Secretary of Education, and distinguished fellow in cultural policy at the conservative Heritage Institute.[11]

Ravitch, Finn, Bennett, and Hirsch are part of an elite conservative educational tradition in the United States. They are also part of a long and ongoing debate about the role of education in American society. Much of this debate, as chronicled by curriculum historians, such as Larry Cuban and Herbert Kliebard, has been over the content of curriculum.[12] In the case of the educational conservatives, it has focused on their critique of progressive education and the work of the philosopher and educator John Dewey.

The conservative educational critique of Dewey and progressive education has a lengthy history. The origins of the debate extend back to the first decades of the twentieth century when figures such as William C. Bagley of the University of Illinois argued against what he identified as "progressive" trends in the educational system that he felt represented an attack on the academic curriculum.[13]

Dewey's work in education began in 1896, when he became a professor at the University of Chicago. In addition to his duties in the departments of philosophy and education, Dewey and his wife Alice opened an experimental laboratory school at the university.[14]

Linking into the progressive reform traditions of the era characterized by figures such as Jane Addams at Chicago's Hull House, Dewey believed that the reform and improvement of education could be brought about through the application of the social sciences, in particular psychology, to the study of schools. Based largely on his experience at the laboratory school, Dewey began to formulate a coherent "progressive" theory of education.

In works such as "My Pedagogic Creed" (1897)[15] and the *School and Society* (1899)[16] Dewey argued that the school should be a social center creating an experience for the child as real and vital as that which they experienced in their homes and families. Dewey's curriculum was highly integrated. Students at the laboratory school would combine writing experiences and working outdoors with subject content in areas such as history, mathematics, and science.

Dewey was more interested in the idea of process and "learning by doing" rather than rote memorization and recitation. He often felt that his ideas were misrepresented by his supposed followers. During the late 1920s Dewey disassociated himself from the Progressive Education Association—a group that had been founded based on his ideas. In 1932 he argued in an article titled "How Much Freedom in the New Schools," published in the *New Republic*, that many progressive educators in their desire to escape an overly formal and regimented curriculum had created in their place programs that reflected their own views and interests rather than an understanding of his work. Dewey supported subject content in instruction, but a subject content that was developmentally appropriate and meaningful for the child.

Although the debate over progressive educational models never really stopped during the early 1930s and 1940s, it was raised to a new level in 1952 with the initiation by Arthur Bestor, Jr., a history professor at the University of Illinois, of the "Life Adjustment" movement in education. Bestor's critique, which began as a journal article,[17] was expanded into a book the following year titled *Educational Wastelands: The Retreat from Learning in Our Public Schools.*[18]

Bestor's work attacked both college and university education schools and the influence of progressive education on the schools at the K-12 level. His criticism focused on the "life adjustment" curriculum, which had been widely adapted in secondary school programs across the country, which emphasized social development and skills over academic content in the curriculum. This curriculum, which focused on having students learn life skills to the detriment of academic areas, although certainly deserving criticism, was not a result of Dewey's model of progressive education. Despite this fact, Dewey was tarred with the same brush by conservatives.

Bestor argued that progressive education had turned into "regressive education."[19] Together with other critics such as Mortimer Smith,[20] Harry J. Fuller,[21] and Albert Lynd,[22] Bestor raised important arguments concerning the failure of contemporary education. Holding Dewey and his progressive philosophy responsible for problems with the public schools, Bestor falsely assumed that Dewey's ideas had in fact come to dominate American public education.

Progressive education itself was by no means a cohesive movement in American education. It represented a number of different strands—several of which Dewey publicly rejected. In fact, it was not the Deweyan educational progressives who had come to dominate American education during the first half of the twentieth century, but the social efficiency experts chronicled by Raymond Callahan in his classic study *Education and the Cult of Efficiency.*[23] As curriculum historian Herbert Kliebard has pointed out, the curriculum of the public schools has historically been a contested territory questioning the purposes of schooling and the actual content of what should be taught. Corporate advocates and efficiency experts, humanists interested in the traditional curriculum, developmentalists, and social meliorists are just a few of the individuals who have vied for control of the American curriculum since the beginning of the twentieth century.[24] Deweyan models of progressive education have by no means been dominant.

By the end of 1957 the national debate on public education was raised to a new level as a result of the launching of the USSR's Sputnik. Educational reform came to be equated with national defense. In 1958 Congress and the Eisenhower administration passed the National Defense Education Act (NDEA), which provided federal funds to improve the academic quality of U.S. schools. Conservative educational forces had come to equate the defense of the country against encroachment by the Russians with the content of the curriculum in the schools.

The rhetoric of war and schooling was reintroduced during the early 1980s under the Reagan administration. In 1983, the U.S. Department of Education released a brief pamphlet titled *A Nation at Risk*. The pamphlet argued that the mediocre quality of our public schools was reducing our economic competitiveness and placing us in severe jeopardy.[25] Educational progress was no longer being realized in our schools. Statistics were presented that led the authors of the report to conclude, "For the first time in the history of our country, the educational skills of one generation will not surpass, will not equal, will not even approach those of their parents."[26]

*A Nation at Risk* was the most influential of a series of reports released in the mid-1980s that called for the reform of public education. Coming from both the public and private sectors, these reports set in motion massive reform at both the federal and the local and state levels. The success of the reforms undertaken as a result of *A Nation at Risk* were limited at best. Attempts to abolish the Department of Education along with the introduction of school prayer and the legalization of tuition tax credits failed. Nonetheless, a conservative educational agenda was set in motion that is continuing to play itself out more than twenty years later.

E. D. Hirsch, Jr., appeared on the school reform scene at almost exactly the same time as the release of *A Nation at Risk*. In December 1981 he had outlined his ideas concerning education and cultural literacy at a conference of the Modern Language Association. An article based on his presentation titled "Cultural Literacy" appeared in the *American Scholar* in 1983.[27] Hirsch subsequently received a letter from Robert Payton, the president of the Exxon Foundation, encouraging him to expand his ideas. In addition, William Bennett, then chairman of the National Endowment for the Humanities and subsequently a secretary of education under Ronald Reagan, came to the support of Hirsch.[28] Funding for the writing of *Cultural Literacy* was provided by Payton and the Exxon Foundation. The book was first published in 1987 by Houghton Mifflin.

## Hirsch's Critique of Dewey

Like other educational conservatives before him, Hirsch sees much of the failure of contemporary education as resulting from the work of John Dewey and the implementation of his ideas concerning progressive education. In this he represents a continuation of the line of thought promoted by Mortimer Smith, Harry J. Fuller, Albert Lynd, and Arthur Bestor.

In *Cultural Literacy* Hirsch launches a critique of Dewey in the first pages of the work that could easily have been written in the early 1950s. Drawing on sources such as Dewey's 1912 *Schools of Tomorrow*, he argues that Dewey believed that "a few direct experiences would suffice to develop the skills children require ... that early education need not be tied to specific content."[29] Hirsch goes on to argue that Dewey, along with figures like the French philosopher Jean Jacques Rousseau, through their advocacy of a content-neutral curriculum, fails to appreciate "the need for the transmission of specific cultural information."[30]

Statements like this convince me that either Hirsch has not read Dewey or has done so very superficially so that he misses much of his essential meaning. In his pivotal 1916 work, *Democracy and Education*, Dewey begins the first chapter of the book with a section he describes as "Renewal of Life by Transmission." In this section he argues that

> Society exists through a process of transmission quite as much as biological life. This transmission occurs by means of

communication of habits of doing, thinking, and feeling from the older to the younger. Without this communication of ideals, hopes, expectations, standards, opinions from those of society who are passing out of group life to those who are coming into it, social life could not survive.[31]

A few paragraphs later, Dewey goes on to argue that there is through the "transmission of ideas and practices the constant reweaving of the social fabric."[32]

Culture for Dewey does not exist without content. The idea of passing knowledge between one generation and another is essential to Dewey. What he argues for is a knowledge that is meaningful to those being taught in the context of their lives in the present. Later in the book, he argues that "The past is a great resource for the imagination; it adds a new dimension to life, but on condition that it be seen as the past of the present, and not as another and disconnected world."[33]

As a result, Dewey would argue that the cultural content and items Hirsch includes in his curriculum have meaning for the learner—if they relate to his or her actual experiences in life. In his 1909 *Moral Principles in Education* Dewey argues that for a child to become a good citizen, training in science, art, and history is absolutely necessary. Nor, as Hirsch maintains, does Dewey reject the accumulation of facts and information, if they have meaning for the learner. For Dewey, there is no motive to studying the past in and of itself. Its value lies in applying its facts and dates to the present.[34]

John Petrovic in an interesting critique of the work of Melanie Phillips talks about how both Phillips and E. D. Hirsch, Jr., misinterpret the work of Dewey. Petrovic points out that for Dewey, piling up information and facts is not necessarily knowledge. According to Petrovic:

> It is this ideal that Dewey applies to all subject matter. German, he points out "is not a fact ... but a mode of social and business intercourse" (1902a, p. 379.) Physics is not about the discovery of important but very remote laws; "it is a set of facts which, through the applications of heat and electricity to our ordinary surroundings, constantly come home to us." (1902a, p. 379)[35]

Dewey in no way rejected the importance of subject matter in the child's learning. What he did do was emphasize that subject matter learned by the child needed to be meaningful.

Hirsch at worst has deliberately distorted the ideas of Dewey and his ideas about schooling. At best, he has been a sloppy scholar. I would like to assume the latter, but there is a clear pattern in his work that suggests a tendency to distort and misrepresent ideas for his own purposes. This is clearly the case with Hirsch's appropriation and use of the work of the Marxist theorist Antonio Gramsci discussed later in this work.

## Who Benefits from Hirsch's Model of Cultural Literacy?

Hirsch believes that the chief beneficiaries of the educational reforms that he advocates are disadvantaged children.[36] He also believes that his proposed reforms will be helpful to children from middle-class homes. According to him: "The educational goal advocated is that of mature literacy for *all* our citizens."[37]

Hirsch's use of the idea of a "mature literacy" for all our citizens is an interesting one. It seems to assume that there is an "immature literacy" at work in our culture as well. Nowhere to my knowledge, is this "immature literacy" actually defined by Hirsch.

For example, in an electronic information and market-oriented culture, is media literacy an "immature" literacy? In an increasingly multicultural and diverse society, is knowledge of Acupuncture, Douglas Addams, Theodor Adorno, affirmative action, Afrocentrism, Aid for Dependent Children, AIDS, the Altair computer, Louis Althusser, the American Association of University Women, anarchy, Maya Angelou, Apple (the corporation), *Art in the Age of Mechanical Reproduction,* the Aspen movie map, Atari, Atavars, authority, and autonomy— just to name a few things that begin with the letter "A"—less important than concepts like those found at the beginning of Hirsch's list like: Hank Aaron, abbreviation, Aberdeen, abolitionism, abortion, absenteeism, absolute monarchy, absolute zero, abstract art, abstract expressionism, academic freedom, a capella, accelerator (particle), accounting, acculturation, Achilles' heel, acid, acquittal, acronym, acrophobia, Acropolis, act of God, or actuary?[38]

Is a quote like "Abandon hope, all ye who enter here," from the beginning of Dante's *Inferno* more meaningful from the viewpoint of being culturally literate than the quote: "The problem of the twentieth century is the problem of the color line" from W. E. B. Du Bois in *The Souls of Black Folk* (1903)? Or the more contemporary quote "The street finds its own uses for things" from William Gibson in *Neuromancer* (1984)? While I am not denying the importance of Dante as a literary and historical figure, are he and his work irrelevant to most people? Is he an author whose ideas are really an important and essential part of the education of all Americans?

Hirsch's model of cultural literacy is based on accumulating a specific store of information. He feels that educators like John Dewey too hastily rejected the idea of "piling up information" as a means of achieving knowledge and meaning. For Hirsch, "Only by piling up specifically shared communal information can children learn to participate in complex cooperative activities with other members of their community."[39]

Hirsch believes that all communities "are founded upon specific shared information."[40] Drawing on what he describes as an "anthropological perspective," he maintains that "the basic goal of education in a human community is acculturation, the transmission to children of the specific information shared by the adults of the group or polis."[41]

This transmission model of education can roughly be equated with Paulo Freire's notion of a "banking model" of education. Hirsch feels that the "progressivists" view the transmission model of schooling in a negative derogatory way.[42] This is despite the fact that figures like John Dewey argued in works such as *Democracy and Education* (1916) that "society not only continues to exist *by* transmission, *by* communication, but it may fairly be said to exist *in* transmission."[43]

The idea that schools conserve a society and its values from one generation to the next through the transmission of values is obvious. We pass on language, political traditions, religious values, and a whole host of other concepts through a natural process of cultural transmission. We have classic books we read, music we listen to, scientific knowledge that we know, and political insights and traditions that are essential to preserving and maintaining our society.

I have no objection—nor do I think most thoughtful educators would—to children learning most of the items included on Hirsch's list. The problem is not whether or not we need to know who Alfred Lord Tennyson was, or the meaning of the term *tit for tat*.[44] The problem is that so many words are not included on Hirsch's list. We must also be concerned about what the words on the list *critically* mean. An educated citizenry—particularly one located in a rapidly changing culture like ours—needs not only to accumulate cultural facts, but cultural meaning. Take an example from recent events: educated citizens, if they are to understand critical aspects of contemporary Muslim culture, need not only to understand that *chadors* and *burkas* are types of veils but their religious significance and their social and cultural implications as well. In other words, facts, although important, may not be sufficient by themselves. We must understand the meaning and significance of the facts as well.

## What Should Be the Aims of Education?

The psychologist Howard Gardner argues that the aims of education should be to produce students "who can think well about the essential questions of human life: who we are, where do we come from, what's the world made of, what have humans achieved and what can we achieve, how does one lead a good life?"[45] For Gardner the "discipline" provides a logical way of organizing knowledge according to specific strategies. Information, including facts and data, are helpful inasmuch as they can inform the critical questions any educated individual should be asking. As Gardner explains: "You cannot think well about a topic or question unless you have information, data, facts. However, that information should not be acquired for its own sake, but as a means of finding a better answer to a consequential question."[46]

Consequential questions of the type Gardner is referring to are typically ones that do not have clear-cut answers and that are open to debate and discussion. They often represent what might be termed the "fault lines of a culture." This fits extremely well with Gerald Graff's argument in *Beyond the Culture Wars: How Teaching the Conflicts Can Revitalize American Education* that if traditional values are being debated, then the debate should be made the focus of instruction.[47] Such an approach not only requires the acquisition of facts and information—key to Hirsch's curricular model—but also their critical interpretation. In doing so, one has the opportunity to reach students on several different levels by employing what James J. O'Donnell believes is "the space of the classroom to teach both the message and the critical reception and evaluation of the message."[48]

O'Donnell refers to the idea of focusing on the debate rather than just the facts as one of "teaching to the surprises." Although it uses many of the same sources, it represents a philosophical approach that is largely in opposition to Hirsch's. As O'Donnell explains:

> The approach I favor to teaching critical reception of teaching the past might best be called "teaching the surprises." To the scholar whose work lies deep within the heartland of Western civilization, the secret truth of the cultural traditions we inherit is that they are so diverse, polymorphous, and surprising. So my teaching strategy starts students where they think they are comfortable and then seeks to disorient and defamiliarize them so that they actually *look* at what they are studying. For a teacher who thinks such moments of epiphany vital to education, such a moment is a godsend.[49]

O'Donnell's approach is slightly different than Graff's in that it not only focuses on critical debates but also consciously tries to "disorient and defamiliarize" students.

Such an approach is closer to that of the radical educator Paulo Freire, who believes that Graff's model of teaching to the conflict "robs students of the opportunity to access critical discourses that will enable them to deconstruct the colonial and hegemonic paradigms, but will also help them realize that one cannot teach the conflict as if, all of a sudden, it fell from the sky. The conflict must be anchored in those competing histories and ideologies that generated the conflict in the first place."[50]

The importance underlying the creation of alternatives lists of words and topics to those of Hirsch lies in their ability, when defined, to anchor the conflicts and issues that form the debate. Words and facts in isolation, and without meaning, are of little use. Hirsch eventually came to recognize this fact by developing various dictionaries of cultural literacy to supplement his initial list.[51] Thus the creation of cultural lists like Hirsch's, as well as the one created for this book, ultimately require the creation of dictionaries to elaborate, define, and contextualize their meaning.

For Hirsch, there is a security in the canon. It is predictable, pleasant, and capable of being controlled. But meaningful learning or "education," as O'Donnell points out, involves "*seeing,* seeing past resemblances to differences, recognizing the otherness of even the familiar."[52]

Teaching the conflicts removes learning from a protected sphere. It confronts, rather than tries to manipulate or control, reality. Referring to university instruction O'Donnell explains:

> There is no refuge from reality in teaching, no orderly life in a kind of Disney World of the mind where nothing really dangerous ever happens and a predictable good time is had by all. School often presents itself to the imagination as that kind of sanitized theme park, but as school becomes university, risks need to be taken. Failure to see this is one of the root causes of our so-called culture wars, where both right and left argue over how to best manage the Disney World University and which exhibits to put on display. In the face of such a spectacle, moderate and practical people turn away, telling their children to study accounting or some other less embattled subject, with the result that the humanities are often held in low esteem.[53]

Avoiding the conflicts and largely just reporting the facts takes the essential elements of learning and makes them what the philosopher Alfred North Whitehead referred to as "inert ideas." As Whitehead argued: "Culture is activity of thought and receptiveness to beauty and human feelings. Scraps of information have nothing to do with it."[54] Ideas that are simply received into the mind without being critically utilized are at best useless. At their worst they can be distracting and possibly destructive.[55]

Teaching the conflicts contradicts Hirsch's conservative educational model. Look, for example, at the following quote by Hirsch included in the preface to *Cultural Literacy:*

> The inherent conservatism of literacy leads to a subtle but unavoidable paradox: the goals of political liberalism require educational conservatism. We make social and economic progress *only* by teaching myths and facts that are predominantly traditional.[56]

I would argue, instead, that true literacy instead requires a *critical literacy*. Such a literacy demands not only knowledge of alternative vocabularies, as well as the history of ideas and conflicts, but also a clear knowledge of theory (ideally rooted in practice) that will allow the framing and interpretation of facts. How, for example, is the construction of race or gender influenced by hegemonic functions or systems in the culture? How does "privilege" shape the experience of people in terms of race, gender, and geographic location? How do schools or families function as systems of cultural reproduction? How does geographic location shape consciousness?

Theory provides us the tools by which to interpret words and definitions we have learned about. Experience in our communities, or through their reconstruction through cultural sources (history, ethnographies, photographs, literature, etc.), makes our ideas "practiced" and real. Questions inevitably follow, as theory interacts with experience.

James J. O'Donnell calls us to "show more imagination than we currently do in our legend making."[57] Do we live in the best of all possible worlds—ones created by our historical heritage and traditions—or do we live in a culture fraught with problems that we inherited from our ancestors? The answer seems obvious—both. As a result, we need to consciously construct a model of culture and history for our schools and the society at large that is both critical and tolerant—critical of lost and suppressed histories and traditions, and tolerant of those groups associated with or benefiting from the oppression.

## Gregory Bateson and the
## "Pattern which Connects"

Alfred North Whitehead argued in *The Aims of Education*, first published in 1929, that the lack of connection or "the fatal disconnection of subjects" is what kills the vitality of the modern curriculum.[58] According to him:

> We offer children Algebra, from which nothing follows:
> Geometry, from which nothing follows; History, from which
> nothing follows; a Couple of Languages, never mastered; and
> lastly, most dreary of all, Literature, represented by the plays
> of Shakespeare, with philological notes and short analyses of
> plot and character to be in substance committed to memory. [59]

Whitehead asks what such lists can have to do with real life. The best that can be said of them is that "it is a rapid table of contents which a deity might run over in his mind while he was thinking of creating a world, and has not yet determined how to put it together."[60]

Whitehead's criticism of the curriculum parallels that of the anthropologist Gregory Bateson. In *Mind and Nature* Bateson raises the disturbing premise that schooling in Europe and America has a consistent tendency to avoid "crucial issues." In a tongue-in-cheek fashion, he asks why the schools avoid addressing questions related to evolution and "social thinking— to daily life and to the eating of breakfast." According to him, most adults—supposedly educated adults—cannot provide their children with

> a reasonable account of concepts such as entropy, sacrament,
> syntax, number, quantity, pattern, linear relation, name, class,
> relevance, energy, redundancy, force, probability, parts,
> whole, information, tautology, homology, mass (either
> Newtonian or Christian), explanation, description, rule of
> dimensions, logical type, metaphor, topology, and so on. What
> are butterflies? What are starfish? What are beauty and
> ugliness?[61]

It is worth noting that only "entropy," "mass" (undifferentiated as to whether it's Newtonian or Christian), "metaphor," "redundancy" and "syntax" are included on Hirsch's list. Why is this the case? Why does Bateson use words and language and why does he pursue concepts and meanings so different from Hirsch? Both are deeply interested in questions of cultural literacy. Why is the vocabulary they use so different? I think the answer lays in the types of questions Bateson feels schools need to have students ask if they are to become educated.

According to Bateson schools provide almost no training concerning "the pattern which connects." It is his conviction that if you "break the pattern which connects the items of learning ... you necessarily destroy all quality." I believe that in this context, "quality" for Bateson refers to the idea of meaningful or important knowledge.

The "pattern which connects," or what I prefer to refer to as the "patterns which connect," include for Bateson what the crab and lobster, the rose and primrose, mean to one another. What do these four life forms mean to the amoeba? to man?[62] In other words, "What is the pattern which connects all the living creatures?"[63]

Bateson is concerned with the fact that our educational system, and in turn our culture, is so little concerned with the "aesthetic." By this he means being "responsive to *the pattern which connects*."[64] It seems to me that what is important in scholarship, as in citizenship and the basic education of our children, is the ability to see the connection between things. When the nineteenth century biologist Haeckel put forward his premise—repeated in most high school and college biology courses—that "ontogeny recapitulates phylogeny," he was demonstrating a remarkable "pattern which connects." In essence, the development of the human embryo in the womb (ontogeny) repeats the evolutionary development of the human species (the phylum) over millions of years.

Good historians representing one important disciplinary area do not simply relate facts and information—a practice that at its worst simply becomes antiquarianism—but they put forth interpretations. Why is it, for example, that revolutions often occur when social conditions improve? Why are revolutions often led by the privileged children of the wealthy and the elite?

Typically useful or meaningful interpretations implied by questions such as these demonstrate a "pattern which connects."

These questions are different from those asked by Hirsch and other cultural conservatives. Hirsch is not interested in having students ask questions or interpret the world as much as he is interested in having them *accept facts* as part of a transmission or banking model of education. Such a model eliminates the elements of critical engagement and dialogue which I believe are essential to any meaningful type of cultural or critical literacy.

## What Hirsch's Curriculum Is Mainly About:
## The Transmission or Banking Model
## of Education and Culture

As mentioned earlier, the idea of a banking or transmission model of education is drawn from the work of the contemporary educational theorist Paulo Freire. According to Freire, under a banking model of education students are considered to be empty containers or vessels into which the teacher, as the agent of the culture, deposits knowledge and information into the learner. Freire believes that in a banking model of education, students do not function critically, but instead, have information imposed on them from the outside. As he explained in *Pedagogy of the Oppressed*:

> To achieve [domination] the oppressors use the banking concept of education in conjunction with a paternalistic social action apparatus within which the oppressed receive the euphemistic title of "welfare recipients." They are treated as individual cases, as marginal persons who deviate from the general configuration of a "good, organized, and just" society. The oppressed are regarded as the pathology of the healthy society, which must therefore adjust these "incompetent and lazy" to its own mentality by changing their mentality…. Translated into practice the concept of banking education is well-suited to the purposes of the oppressors, whose tranquility rests on how well humans fit the world the oppressors have created, and how little they question it.[65]

Rather than a banking or transmission model of knowledge, I believe that a more democratic and critical model of culture is called for. Stanley Aronowitz and Henry A. Giroux, for example, call for "a definition of culture as a set of activities by which different groups produce collective memories, knowledge, social relations, and values within historically constituted relations of power."[66] For Aronowitz and Giroux, "culture is about the production and legitimation of particular ways of life."[67] They argue clearly that schools often transmit cultural values and norms that are highly specific in terms of race, gender, and economic class. Hirsch seems to have no understanding of the relationship of his work to ideas such as these—he has no understanding, or his ideas leave no room for a concept such as this. One wonders if his ideas on education are driven largely by a secular faith he has constructed out of the Western canon, rather than by a critical understanding of education, race, gender, and economic class in American culture.

In Hirsch's approach, minority students sign away their cultural heritage in order to be able to enter into the mainstream culture. There is no notion on Hirsch's part that by accepting the cultural definitions identified by him in works like *Cultural Literacy*, the minority student may be resisting domination by the mainstream culture. For Hirsch, such a rejection of the mainstream culture on the part of a minority student is an act of ignorance—an act of cultural suicide—or a failure on the part of the student to identify what meaningful knowledge is actually about.

Hirsch assumes that minority children will readily embrace the mainstream culture and its canon. This idea flies in the face of much of what we know about how cultural minorities respond to mainstream culture. Paul Willis's classic study, *Learning to Labor*, suggests, for example, that there is often a great deal of resistance to the attempts of schools to impose specific cultural and class-oriented values on students. Willis discovered that nonacademically oriented working-class English adolescents consciously rejected the values emphasized as part of the traditional schooling process. In doing so, they asserted their own identities and the traditions of their social group.[68]

Hirsch's assumption that minority students will readily embrace mainstream cultural values has me recalling Henry Giroux's description of growing up in a working-class neighborhood in Providence, Rhode Island. According to Giroux, the cultural messages that he received through the curriculum were alien to him:

> It was like being sent to a strange planet. Teaching was exclusively centered on obscure books and the culture of print. Desire was mainly a male prerogative reserved for sports during recess time. The language we learned and had to speak was different, strange, and unusually verbose. Bodily and intellectual memories disappeared for working-class kids in this school. We were on a different train, one oriented toward a cheap imitation of the knowledge of high culture. Latin, Western civilization, math, spelling, social studies, and religion were given to us through force-feeding methods that characterized public schools for kids who had little hope of leaving their neighborhood, even if they graduated.[69]

For Giroux, what he learned had little to do with where he and his classmates came from, "who we were, or where we thought, at least, we were going."[70] Films, books, journals, videos, and music did much more to shape him than did his formal education.[71]

In reading Hirsch and many of the other cultural conservatives like him, one is led to believe that the knowledge they promote is noble, altruistic, and neutral. As Joe Kincheloe and Shirley Steinberg argue, this type of "view dismisses the cultural and power-related dimensions of knowledge."[72]

## Hirsch's Model as Representing a Type of Cultural Imperialism or Educational Colonialism

Cultural imperialism is a concept that has been widely discussed in the educational literature since the mid-1970s. Martin Carnoy, for example, in his *Education as Cultural Imperialism* (1974) argues that Western education, far from acting as a liberating force in the Third World, "came to most countries as part of imperialist domination."[73] Formal education was used as a means of imperial domination and control. According to Carnoy, "imperial powers attempted through schooling to train the colonized for roles that suited the colonizer."[74]

Other researchers have demonstrated at length how colonial models of education have worked. In two relatively recent and very powerful works, John Willinsky's *Learning to Divide the World: Education at Empire's End* (1998) and Linda Tuhiwai Smith's *Decolonizing Methodologies: Research and Indigenous Peoples* (1999), clear evidence is provided to demonstrate how colonialist models of education were part of the imperialist machinery of Africa, Asia, and the Australian subcontinent.[75]

According to Carnoy, cultural imperialism colonizes knowledge itself in such a way that it "perpetuates the hierarchical structure of society."[76] Carnoy maintains that seemingly disinterested groups who supported education in colonial systems as a means to social mobility were often serving their own economic and social interests, or "were themselves colonized sufficiently to accept the system's rules for limited self-criticism."[77]

Colonialist models of education not only apply to historically colonized societies but also to economic and racial groups in a culture such as the United States. The effects of such models, whether as part of a historical colonial system such as Victorian England, or as part of a system of racial or class domination like that of the United States throughout most of its history, are devastating. Linda Tuhiwai Smith, an indigenous scholar from Australia (Ngati Awa and Ngati Poru) suggests that imperialist systems deny the colonized their "claims to humanity, to having a history, and to all sense of hope."[78]

Cultural imperialism, whether it is acted out on the stage of empire or by emeritus English professors in the hallways of American universities, has the effect of marginalizing individuals and their cultural meaning and identity. Cultural imperialism assumes that one social group's experience—in this case what John Fiske refers to as the "power bloc"—is the norm for everyone else. According to Joe Kincheloe and Shirley Steinberg:

> In this context, the power bloc consolidates its ability to regulate subordinate groups by framing their differences as deficiencies.... Such a process highlights the culturally

imperialistic power bloc's capacity for making meaning for the society at large. Such power is a form of hermeneutic domination that privileges the experiences, values, cultural capital, and viewpoints of the dominant group.[79]

Hirsch imposes his worldview—perhaps well-meaningly, but certainly self-servingly—in ways that deny the rights and perspectives of others, particularly those who are culturally, socially, economically, and politically different from him.

Typically, Hirsch cloaks his opinions and proposals in a misconstrued rhetoric of democracy and egalitarianism. For Hirsch, inequality can only be addressed if minority groups are fully integrated into a system of shared democratic knowledge; that is, in Jeffersonian terms, a "common curriculum." In *The Schools We Need*, Hirsch quotes a declaration of principles issued in 1994 by the Parliament of Norway, to the effect that:

> Common background knowledge is thus at the core of a national network of communication between members of a democratic community. It makes it possible to fathom complex messages and to interpret new ideas, situations and challenges. Education plays a leading role in passing on this common background information—the culture everybody must be familiar with if society is to remain democratic and its citizens sovereign. [80]

What Hirsch does not take into account is the issue of whether shared systems of knowledge can be used simply to dominate and control while in the process of reproducing and perpetuating specific class and social structures.

This of course, is the fundamental idea underlying imperialistic or colonialist educational models. Such models, according to Gail Kelly and Phillip Altbach, manifest themselves in a number of different ways. In a traditional colonial setting schools emerge that in most instances "reflect the power and the needs of the colonizers."[81] Typically, the aspirations, traditional cultures, knowledge systems, and needs of those being dominated are ignored.

In a colonized educational system the individual becomes increasingly alienated from his native culture. Colonized individuals are directed. They do not direct themselves. Their creative power is impaired. They are objects, not subjects. Contemporary educational critics, including Martin Carnoy, Joe Kincheloe, Peter McLaren, Joel Spring, and Shirley Steinberg have all argued that throughout their history, public schools in the United States have attempted to colonize many of the groups whom they teach. In particular, the experiences of women, blacks, and Native Americans (Indians) have often been cited as a demonstration of a colonial system of education at work in American society.[82]

Hirsch's model of "cultural literacy" certainly can be viewed in a colonial or imperialistic context. Consider for a moment some of the major points made by Kelly and Altbach about colonialist educational systems:

1. that those who are colonized are considered intellectually, physically, and morally inferior when compared with the colonizers.

2. that colonial education is controlled by the colonizer and is detached from both the educational system of the colonizer and the colonized.

3. that the history of the colonized group is denied or reinterpreted in such a way that the fundamental identity of the colonized group is significantly obscured or diminished.

4. that the content of colonial education is different from that given the colonizer.

5. that the colonized group eventually comes to identify with the values and beliefs of the colonizer and to assume their superiority.[83]

Now consider how they fit Hirsch's model of cultural literacy:

To begin with, Hirsch considers individuals outside of the elite Western cultural tradition to be inferior—not simply different. Without knowledge of the Western tradition, disadvantaged children are doomed to a life with limited options and opportunities. According to him:

> Cultural literacy constitutes the only sure avenue of
> opportunity for disadvantaged children, the only reliable way
> of combating the social determinism that now condemns them
> to remain in the same social and educational condition of their
> parents.[84]

Poverty for Hirsch is a direct result of cultural illiteracy. He consistently underplays the notion that it might be a result of systematic prejudice or social, economic, or political exploitation.

According to Hirsch, "Only by accumulating shared symbols, and the shared information that the symbols represent, can we learn to communicate effectively with one another in our national community."[85] Of course Hirsch, almost as matter of faith, assumes that the elite Western cultural traditional is the only meaningful system of knowledge for an educated citizenry.

He does not consider the possibility that an educated citizenry can be diverse and can engage in a critical dialogue involving different perspectives and experiences. Because someone is not part of the Western elite tradition does not necessarily mean that they are inferior. For example, Native American traditions of valuing the land for its physical and spiritual worth, rather than as a source of business exploitation, and the importance they placed on the group rather than on the individual, are certainly alternative ways of viewing culture from which Western elite culture might learn a great deal.

In this context, the Western canon is an important and valuable body of knowledge—one that is essential to our understanding of who we are as Americans. But it is not the only body of cultural knowledge our children need to know—nor, as pointed out above, is it necessarily always the best. It is clear that as a body of knowledge, many of its assumptions need to be challenged if we are to achieve a more just and equitable society.

By limiting his list of culturally relevant terms and issues, Hirsch fulfills the third characteristic of Kelly and Altbach's model of a colonized educational system by denying the history of subjugated groups, or, in certain instances, reinterpreting their history.

Hirsch argues that a common core of knowledge is essential to all educated citizens. This model does not fit the fourth point in Kelly and Altbach's model, which maintains that "the content of colonial education is different from that given the colonizer." The problem, however, is that Hirsch's common core of knowledge is restricted to one cultural group and its traditions. It feeds into and reinforces the fifth point in their model, in which "the colonized group eventually comes to identify with the values and beliefs of the colonizer and to assume their superiority." Hirsch's model, in fact, promotes precisely this end.

Kelly and Altbach's arguments clearly conform to the educational experience of various minority groups in American culture. Take, for example, the case of the African-American population, which demonstrates each of their points:

1. Until recently, and unfortunately still in many instances, the dominant white culture has considered itself superior in almost every way to African American culture.

2. African American students have only recently been integrated into the general educational system of the culture.

3. Until the 1960s the contributions made by blacks to American culture and society were rarely recognized or discussed.

4. The type of education provided to blacks was frequently different from, and most often inferior to, that provided in the mainstream school system.

5. As a result of the tradition of domination and oppression many blacks have looked upon the mainstream white culture as being superior to their own.

Certainly the inequities of the educational system are fewer than they were a generation ago. The desegregation of schools and the passage of the various civil rights acts of the 1960s have greatly expanded the possibilities for genuine equality in our society. Yet there is also the fact that discrimination can also function at a very subtle and sometimes almost undetectable level. One can see this in the case of cultural hegemony.

## Hirsch's Model and Cultural Hegemony

Hegemony is a concept that was first developed by the Italian Marxist theorist Antonio Gramsci (1891–1937). For Gramsci, hegemony represented the diffusion or permeation throughout the culture of a specific system of values, attitudes, and beliefs that had the effect of supporting the existing power structure in the culture.

> Hegemony in this sense might be defined as an "organizing principle" that is diffused by the process of socialization into every area of daily life. To the extent that this prevailing consciousness is internalized by the population it becomes part of what is generally called "common sense" so that the philosophy, culture, and morality of the ruling elite comes to appear as the natural order of things.[86]

According to educational and cultural theorist Peter McLaren:

> Hegemony refers to the maintenance of domination not by the sheer exercise of force *but primarily through consensual social practices, social forms, and social structures produced in specific sites such as the church, the state, the school, the mass media, the political system and the family.* ... Hegemony refers to the moral and intellectual leadership of a dominant class over a subordinate class achieved not through coercion (i.e., threat of imprisonment or torture) or the willful construction of rules and regulations (as in a dictatorship or fascist regime), but rather through the general winning of consent of the subordinate class to the authority of the dominant class.[87]

Hegemony is particularly interesting since the very people whom it oppresses often embrace it. As a result, they unconsciously contribute to their own oppression.

In the context of Hirsch, hegemonic systems set the character and content of discourse in a culture. They do this, according to Douglas Kellner, in that they "define the limits of discourse, by setting the political agenda, by defining the issues and terms of debate, and by excluding oppositional ideas."[88] Such efforts often meet with resistance.

Thus, even though a hegemonic system is in place, it does not mean that it is necessarily accepted. At the same time, organizing or sometimes even being aware of the need for resistance is difficult for oppressed groups to do. One of the most common places for resistance is found in popular culture. Songs, movies, clothing, and other cultural representations act as a means by which to protest or promote an alternative model. Often what is perceived as being "uncultured" is instead a representation of an articulate and meaningful oppositional culture.

Hirsch shows no awareness in his work that rather than being neutral and objective, his choice of curriculum is highly selective and reflective of a dominant cultural hegemony. Nowhere in *Cultural Literacy* or *The Schools We Need* does he recognize that systems of canonical knowledge have often been used as a means to dominate and control subordinate cultures. Although Hirsch believes that there is power to be gained from a mastery of selected facts and information, he has no insight into the fact that such systems of knowledge can exclude and discourage potentially critical and alternative ways of constructing the world.

This idea of teaching students to understand the power interests within canonical systems of knowledge is critical. I think back, for example, to my own privileged education in a high school in the mid-1960s. I was a teacher's son at an elite private school in upstate New York. My high school American history course was superbly taught. There were no questions about what was appropriate knowledge for us to learn. We used a textbook that included no references to black history, except in the context of slavery or figures like Booker T. Washington and George Washington Carver. I learned about figures like W. E. B. Du Bois by reading about him outside of class. Eldridge Cleaver and the Black Power Movement were introduced to me outside of the traditional curriculum.

I remember a visiting black scholar from the University of Buffalo coming over to the school to talk with us, and how I asked him how it was possible for there to be black history when there were no written records left by black people. It is hard to believe that I could have ever asked a question so seemingly naive, except for the fact that it reflected the Eurocentric tradition in which I had been educated.

Likewise, women were excluded from my early historical training. Other than brief mention of the suffrage movement, I have no memory in my courses in high school of reading or learning anything about the role of women in American history and culture. The education I was being given was considered among the best in the region. I did well on my college entrance exams, went to a good university, and continued to receive a fairly narrow training focused almost entirely on the Western canonical tradition.

Being educated in a closed system, I did not know much about other traditions. On the rare occasions I was introduced to these traditions, I dismissed them as secondary, trivial, or not holding the substance of the works from the Western canon. Thus *Aesop's Fables* held more validity for me than the Central African tales of Anansi the Spiderman or the Jataka tales from India. In the case of the Anansi stories, no one bothered to show me that they were the basis for many of the traditional folk tales like Br'er Rabbit that came out of the South in the second half of the nineteenth century. I had no knowledge of these traditions as part of my early education. It was, in fact, only as part of my graduate education that I discovered that these other stories and traditions from Africa and Asia were in fact the foundation for much of the Western European Aesopic tradition.

In my high school education, the European exploration of the world was emphasized. I had no idea, for example, that seven times between 1405 and 1433 great Chinese armadas loaded with silk, porcelain, and lacquer ware traveled from China to Ceylon, Arabia, and East Africa to trade for spices, ivory, medicines, rare woods, and pearls. These armadas, which at their largest included nearly 30,000 men and dozens of ships, included gigantic nine-masted junks measuring as large as 400 feet long and 150 feet wide. These boats, among the largest wooden vessels ever built, dwarfed European craft of the period. Christopher Columbus's largest ship, the *Santa Maria*, for example, measured a mere 90 by 30 feet and his crew numbered only ninety persons.

Why is it that when I was introduced to the great European explorations, beginning with the Portuguese trips to India and Africa, I was not also told about the Chinese and their exploits during the same period and their travel to many of the same locations? Why are these and similar stories not part of most American children's study of European history?[89]

Why is it that although I learned about the Holocaust and the murder of 6 million Jews during World War II, I never learned anything about the genocide under the Belgian rule of King Leopold II? Was the murder of somewhere between 5 and 8 million in the Congo region of Africa between 1885 and 1908 less important than the Nazi Holocaust?[90]

Whose history gets told, as has been argued throughout this book, is a negotiated process. It changes as individuals gain greater recognition and power in a culture. I began to learn black history because activists in the civil rights movement demanded change in our culture, which eventually came to be reflected in the content of curriculum—curriculum that I learned as a student. As a result, my view of the world was profoundly changed.

I refer to my personal experience because I think it points to how potentially closed and limited educational models like those proposed by Hirsch and other conservatives can be. Hirsch seems to have no idea that his theories potentially enforce a null curriculum, in other words, a curriculum that teaches that certain cultures, people, or ideas are not important or significant, by not including them in the curriculum.

## Hirsch and the "Null Curriculum"

The curriculum theorist Elliot Eisner (1985) defines the null curriculum by the seeming paradox that we teach something by not teaching it. Eisner categorizes the null curriculum along two major dimensions: the cognitive processes that are stressed and disregarded and the subject matter included or excluded in curricula. The null curriculum has serious implications for him in that it affects the types of options one is able to consider as a learner, the vantage points from which one can view a situation or problem, and the alternatives one can consider. According to him, serious consequences for schools result not only "by virtue of what they do teach, but also by virtue of what they neglect to teach."[91]

By choosing certain content, we make clear cultural and political statements about what is of significance to us as a society. Traditional mores and values are sustained and stabilized via the null curriculum. Hirsch maintains that selection is an essential part of defining any curriculum. It is the premise underlying his entire approach. It is not clear that he understands the significance of his not choosing an item and its implications in terms of the null curriculum.

Hirsch, in his disregard of the critical and cultural studies literature in education, makes no reference to the idea of curriculum representing a type of cultural capital. Hirsch in no way acknowledges the null curriculum or the fact that his Core Knowledge Curriculum as he conceives it, can function to promote a null curriculum and in turn the purposeful and deliberate exclusion of the perspectives, issues, and histories of specific populations and cultures that constitute—at least in part—the American people. When he does include these perspectives, it is only minimally and often done in patriarchal tone. As he explains in his new preface to the 1987 edition of *Cultural Literacy*, the conservatism of literate culture need not be total.

> New elements are constantly coming in, and old ones falling away from use. Americans are right to press for reforms such as greater representation of women and minorities and of non-Western cultures, and to insist that literate culture keep up with historical and technical change.[92]

Having said this, he goes on in the following sentence to explain that less than 20 percent of the items on his list are of recent origin, and that "80 percent of the listed items have been in use for more than a hundred years!"[93]

The fact that Hirsch disregards the critical and cultural studies literature in education does not mean that he does not use its major theoreticians for his own purposes. This is blatantly so in his adoption of the work of the Italian cultural theorist Antonio Gramsci.

## Hirsch and the Appropriation of Gramsci

Antonio Gramsci is widely recognized as one of the leading Marxist theorists of the twentieth century. Born in Sardinia in 1891, he eventually settled in the northern Italian industrial city of Turin. The founder of the Italian Communist Party, which he began to lead in 1924, he was imprisoned in 1926 by Mussolini's fascist regime. Gramsci died in 1937, the day after his release from prison. Much of his work, which was written in and smuggled out of prison, deals with issues of culture, civil society, education, and hegemony. For Gramsci, culture and power were critically connected in society, as were knowledge and power. [94]

Gramsci being one of the leading radical theorists of the twentieth century, it is rather remarkable to find E. D. Hirsch, Jr. using his work as a justification for ideas on cultural literacy and education. Hirsch maintains in *The Schools We Need* that Gramsci, in his opposition to the fascist educational system under Mussolini, rejected progressivism in education. According to Hirsch, Gramsci

> held that political progressivism demanded educational conservatism. The oppressed class should be taught to master the tools of power and authority—the ability to read and write, and communicate—and to gain enough traditional knowledge to understand the worlds of nature and the culture surrounding them. [95]

Hirsch's use of Gramsci is based on the work of Harold Entwhistle, a British theorist and the author of *Antonio Gramsci: Conservative Schooling for Radical Politics.*[96] Hirsch's discussion is limited to a couple of pages at the beginning of *The Schools We Need*, in which he seems to be asserting that Gramsci distrusted the ideas of Mussolini's educational minister Giovanni Gentile, who evidently was incorporating progressive models into his reformulation of Italian schools. Specifically, Hirsch quotes Gramsci about these schools to the following effect:

The new concept of schooling is in its romantic phase, in which the replacement of "mechanical" by natural methods has become unhealthily exaggerated ... previous pupils at least acquired a certain baggage on concrete facts. Now there will no longer be any baggage to put in order.... The most paradoxical aspect of it all is that this new type of school is advanced as being democratic, while it in fact is destined not merely to perpetuate social differences, but crystallize them in Chinese complexities.[97]

Henry Giroux accuses both Hirsch and Entwhistle of selectively reading Gramsci. Hirsch's use of Gramsci is particularly curious. He draws on the single quote cited above taken from Gramsci's *Prison Notebooks.*[98] Using this quote, he co-opts Gramsci as a theorist for his conservative educational agenda.

Hirsch is so impressed by Gramsci's quote that he ends up dedicating *The Schools We Need* to him. Yet, a more careful reading of Gramsci suggests that he would in fact be in opposition to the essential characteristics of Hirsch's model of cultural literacy. As Gramsci explains in *The Prison Notebooks:*

We must break the habit of thinking that culture is encyclopedic knowledge whereby man [sic] is viewed as a mere container in which to pour and conserve empirical data or brute disconnected facts which he will have to subsequently pigeonhole in his brain as in the columns of a dictionary so as to be able to eventually respond to the varied stimuli of the external world. This form of education is especially harmful, especially to the proletariat. It only serves to create misfits, people who believe themselves superior to the rest of humanity because they have accumulated in their memory a certain quantity of facts and dates which they cough up at every opportunity to almost raise a barrier between themselves and others.[99]

In his critique of Hirsch's use—perhaps misappropriation would be a better term—of Gramsci in *The Schools We Need*, Henry Giroux argues that: "Hirsch's 'discovery' that Gramsci is actually a poster boy for conservative thought combines the bad faith of misrepresentation with the reductionism of an ideological fervor that seems to make a mockery of political sense and historical accuracy."[100] For Giroux, the "bounds of plausibility" are stretched by Hirsch's scholarship, which aligns conservative educational thinkers such as Charles Sykes and Diane Ravitich. As Giroux explains: "Not only does such an appropriation represent a form of theoretical disingenuousness and political opportunism, it is also an affront to everything that Gramsci stood for as a renegade Marxist revolutionary."[101]

If a scholar is to venture outside of his or her discipline, then he or she has an obligation to be reasonably familiar with the literature and the knowledge of the field upon which he or she is exploring or commenting. This means understanding a field's history as well as its theoretical assumptions. Although this scholar has every right to reject interpretations, to provide alternative explanations, and to critique what a field is about, he does not have the right to distort the knowledge within a field without being severely criticized. While Hirsch cloaks himself in the highest possible academic standards, when people with significant training in educational theory, history, and philosophy—that is, the social foundations of education—review his work, he is consistently criticized for its poor quality.

Among those who are highly critical of Hirsch and his work are the educational philosopher Maxine Greene,[102] Stanley Aronowitz and Henry Giroux,[103] Edgar Schuster,[104] Walter Feinberg,[105] Kristen L. Buras,[106] and Richard Ognibene.[107] Their critiques include not only the ideological and philosophical assumptions of Hirsch, but also the care and quality of his research. In their review of Hirsch's *Cultural Literacy*, Stanley Aronowitz and Henry Giroux, for example, criticize Hirsch for ignoring in his analysis how schools function as agencies of social and cultural reproduction, their discrimination against minority children through various approaches to reading, his lack of awareness of how schools silence and discriminate against students, and his lack of understanding of how "state and other social, economic, and political interests bear down on and shape the daily practices of school organization and classroom life."[108]

Trying to tell Hirsch that he needs to listen to the scholars in educational research who represent the social foundations is almost certainly a futile effort. He, in fact, holds them along with the faculties who teach in American schools of education as being largely responsible for the problems of American education. In *Cultural Literacy* he argues, for example, in Chapter 5 that: "We have too readily blamed shortcomings in American education on social changes (the disorientation of the American family or the impact of television) or incompetent teachers or structural flaws in our school systems. But the chief blame should fall on faulty theories promulgated in our schools of education and accepted by educational policymakers."[109]

This is an old, grossly inaccurate, and tired argument that goes back at least to the late 1940s and early 1950s. In *The Schools We Need* Hirsch draws on Arthur Bestor, Jr.'s earlier referenced argument that there is an "interlocking public school directorate" that dominates American public education. Hirsch quotes one of Bestor's key assertions from his 1953 book *Educational Wastelands:*

> The members of these committees and commissions, the men and women actively engaged in questionnaire making, curriculum outlining, and propagandizing, are drawn almost exclusively from three interrelated professional groups. First of all there are professors of education in universities, colleges, and normal schools. Second, there are super-intendents, principals, and other local public administrators and supervisors. Third, there are officials, "experts," and other bureaucrats in the state departments of public instruction and the federal office of education. These three groups, collectively known as professional educationists, have drawn together in recent years into what amounts to an interlocking public school directorate.[110]

Bestor's arguments, now more than a half-century old, were suspect and highly debatable when he made them. They are even more so now, as they carry intellectual echoes of McCarthyism and the "witch hunts" of the early and mid-1950s.

Anyone who works in a school of education in the United States is profoundly aware of the extent to which the curriculum of the public schools is not under the control of the education professorate. Curricula are controlled at the local and state level. Requirements for teacher certification come through national associations like the National Council for Accreditation of Teacher Education (NCATE) and through guidelines put in place by state departments of education—typically under the direction of state legislators who create law and control finances.

Schools of education are among the most diverse and interdisciplinary units to be found in American universities. A typical school can have specialists in curriculum, curriculum theory, the history of education, special education, educational psychology, teaching of English as a second language, bilingual education, educational technology, adult education, reading, vocational education, sports science and kinesiology, school counseling, educational measurement, and so on. Rivalries between units are often enormous, as are methodological differences. For the past twenty-five years, for example, a major and ongoing debate has taken place in most schools over the value of quantitative versus qualitative models of research. The debate is far from being resolved. Whatever schools of education are, they are not uniform places in which there is a consensus on either how research should be done or what the primary focus and purpose of education should be.

And yet Hirsch would have the general reader believe that schools of education are part of an "impregnable fortress" of interlocking educational systems that extend up to the state and even national level. Consider the following quote Hirsh uses from the conservative educator Mortimer Smith's 1949 book, *And Madly Teach:*

> If anyone will take the trouble to investigate, it will be found that those who make up the staffs of the schools of colleges of education, and the administrators and teachers whom they train to run the system, have a truly amazing uniformity of opinion regarding the aims, the content, and the methods of education. They constitute a cohesive body of believers with a clearly formulated set of dogmas and doctrines, and they are perpetuating the faith by seeing to it through state laws and the rules of state departments of education that only those teachers and administrators are certified who have been trained in correct dogma.[111]

The supposed monopolistic control of the public schools by schools of education is sustained through their power to certify teachers. According to Hirsch: "Education schools and their allies in state departments of education perpetuate themselves by requiring prospective teachers to take a specified number of courses ... in order to be credentialed."[112]

If Hirsch were to check certification requirements in almost any state, if he were to consult with the people who teach and research in schools and colleges of education, he would realize the absurdity of his position. Education programs are under extraordinary pressure from state departments of education to conform with curriculum standards that largely contradict progressive aims and purposes of education. As Kristen L. Buras points out: "The courses required for professional teacher certification are not predominantly grounded in progressive philosophy. Rather, the work is largely focused upon the psychology of learning, classroom management, educational standards, assessment, and subject matter."[113] Hirsch's assessment of the control of the state certification by schools and colleges of education is simply false. I challenge him to show any evidence that such a model is actually at work by looking at state department of education teacher certification requirements and how they are created.

Misrepresentation of this type is found throughout Hirsch's writing on education. It is remarkable that general reviewers of Hirsch and his work have not taken him more to task for his sources. It is as though nothing has happened in the field of education research and teacher education in more than fifty years. Note the following quote Hirsch draws from Bestor's 1953 *Educational Wastelands*:

> One of the most shocking facts about the field of education is the almost complete absence of rigorous criticism from within. The paean of praise that greets every novel proposal, the closing of ranks that occur whenever a word of criticism is spoken from the outside and ... the extreme unwillingness of professional educationists to submit their proposal to free public discussion and honest criticism frequently assumes the even uglier form of showering critics, no matter how upright and well-informed, with vituperation and personal abuse.[114]

The ongoing debate in reading about the use of whole language versus phonics, the revisionist and radical revisionist movement of the 1960s and 1970s in educational history, the emergence of critical theory, cultural studies, and postmodern theory in the 1980s, the more recent debates over national standards in math and social studies, merit pay, the professionalization of teaching, school-based management, critical thinking, psychological testing, AIDS and sex education, the validity of I.Q. and standardized testing, the appropriate uses of educational technology and the nature and meaning of literacy, including cultural literacy, to name just a few—all highly contested within the field of educational research and teacher education—are treated by Hirsch as though they have never existed.

Hirsch believes that the source of the supposed intellectual uniformity of American education emanates from a single institution: Teachers College, Columbia University. According to him: "From Teachers College, Columbia University, there occurred a quasibiological propagation of ideas through which the intellectual DNA of the parent institution in New York was implanted in daughter institutions, and thereafter continued to be replicated from one education school to another. By now, most education professors, and most students taught by them, are the intellectual children, grandchildren, or even great-grandchildren of Teachers College, Columbia University."[115]

Hirsch extends his critique of Dewey and progressive education by maintaining that Teacher's College—particularly through the efforts of figures such as William Heard Kilpatrick and other Deweyans, hijacked American educational reform in the early part of this century and imposed on it a set of progressive and child-centered values that have crippled its potential and possibilities. Nothing could be farther from the truth. True Deweyan models of education are not to be found in most public schools in the United States. Ironically enough, if they exist anywhere it is in a limited number of elite private and university laboratory schools populated almost exclusively by the children of the wealthy and the elite. I challenge Hirsch and his followers to show me where true progressive models of education are to be found in American schools; that is, ones that follow the types of standards Dewey established at the laboratory school at University of Chicago in the early 1890s. I would suggest that they will find instead a U.S. school system that employs an overly mechanistic curriculum taught by repetition and that is too often more interested in the control and management of the child rather than his or her personal discovery and liberation.

## Hirsch and Scientific Standards

Hirsch cloaks a great deal of his educational writing in references to science and to what is understood by psychologists. In a thoughtful review by the educational and developmental psychologist Michael Pressley, Hirsch is taken to task for his lack of experience actually researching and observing in school settings.[116] Pressley also takes Hirsch to task for not adequately demonstrating that the models he is employing in his core knowledge schools are, in fact, effective. As Pressley explains, "I was hoping for a book that told much about these schools, especially how the core knowledge perspective was translating into practice."[117] Instead, according to Pressley, what is put forward is "a wholesale attack on educational progressivism."[118]

Hirsch's use of psychology to support his position in both *Cultural Literacy* and *The Schools We Need* seems extreme, narrow, and limited. Although the author of this monograph has had three or four courses in developmental and educational psychology as part of his undergraduate training, I do not feel sufficiently versed in the literature to do the sort of detailed critique provided by Pressley. He does feel comfortable challenging Hirsch's use of scientific and elite publications to justify his position on education.

In Hirsch's response to what I consider a balanced and fair review of *The Schools We Need* written by Walter Feinberg, a professor of Educational Foundations at the University of Illinois, he accuses Feinberg of portraying him as an "anti-education-school 'fundamentalist' and a control freak."[119] Whether or not Hirsch is a control freak is not something that can be accurately determined from his work. What can be analyzed is his occasionally absurd, and from a research point of view, bizarre arguments.

In his response to Feinberg, for example, Hirsch calls on educational researchers working in education schools to call on "consensus" and "mainstream" science to prove the validity and soundness of their research. Hirsch explains his view as follows:

> Briefly, I would define mainstream science as the most widely accepted work that gets published in the most rigorous scientific journals, no matter where the researchers are themselves located. For instance, an inference drawn by an education professor in a highly refereed article published in *Science* is more reliable than a contrary inference drawn by an education professor or, indeed, by anyone else in a less rigorous venue. The reason for this consistent (although not absolute) distinction in reliability is that a rigorous publication venue filters out a lot of second-rate science—of which there is certainly no shortage outside of education schools.[120]

Such an idea is nothing short of absurd. In the paragraph following the one quoted above, Hirsch describes himself as having nothing but the warmest praise for the work of the psychologist Jerome Bruner.[121] This comment in itself is curious, since so much of Bruner's work, like his curriculum "Man: A Course of Study," would seem to be a continuation of Dewey's notion of learning through active participation and doing. But putting this aside, if one follows Hirsch's logic, psychologists like Bruner (who by the way has spent much of his career teaching in education schools), would be well served if they published most of their research in scientific journals almost completely detached from their field.

Why should the editors and reviewers of a scientific journal like *Science* know any more about educational psychology than the editors and reviewers in the *Journal of Educational Psychology*? Why are largely experimental models of hard science considered appropriate to judge issues involving educational research and psychology? Why should an editor who is an expert in quantum physics or cellular biology have any knowledge to make judgments outside of his or her field? Jean Piaget, arguably the greatest psychologist of child development and learning in the twentieth century, conducted what were essentially qualitative observational studies of children. They were not scientific in the sense of the hard science to which Hirsch seems to be referring.

I would have Hirsch consider whether or not historians, or literary theorists like him, should also submit their work to the scrutiny and review of scientific researchers such as those whose work appears in the pages of journals such as *Science.* Although I suspect that he would argue that such an idea is absurd, I likewise would argue that anyone who knows anything about the complex and interdisciplinary field of education would argue that what he proposes is nothing less than ridiculous.

### Are American Schools a Failure?

Hirsch makes the remarkable argument that "Although our political traditions and even our universities may be without peer, our K-12 education is among the least effective in the developed world."[122] While there is much that is admirable about the American political system, we must also ask about its limitations. Why, for example, do we have the tenth highest infant mortality rate in the industrialized world? Why do we still have such high levels of poverty? Why do we have an ongoing problem with violence and crime? Why do so many of our communities seem devoid of any sense of identity and purpose?

At the same time, how can it be that our K-12 schools are so poor and universities and colleges so excellent? Aren't the students who populate those colleges and universities the very ones who graduated from the K-12 schools? Or, are the people who attend our colleges and universities actually better prepared than Hirsch maintains?

One possibility that seems very real is that our educational system is inherently unequal, serving certain groups much better than others. Hirsch fails to address this issue, just as he fails to engage in the actual debate about whether test scores have declined in recent years. Richard Rothstein, an education writer for the *New York Times,* makes a convincing argument that Americans have for at least 100 years ritualistically complained that the public schools were not doing the job that they needed to. The evidence he assembles, which seems consistent with that of other researchers, is that there has never been a golden age of public schooling. We are probably doing as well as we ever have with public education. Although this may not be good enough, it is not that the school system is in decline.

Researchers like David Berliner and Bruce Biddle maintain that there is a "manufactured crisis" in education. Looking historically at test scores, they argue that there has not been—as popularly reported in the press—a decline in test scores over the past generation, that today's students are out-achieving their parents academically, and that American students actually stand up well on comparative international measures. According to Berliner and Biddle, much of the criticism of public education in recent years has been politically motivated by educational conservatives interested in "scapegoating educators" in order to serve their political agenda.[123]

Berliner and Biddle's work has been criticized by a number of individuals including the educational researcher Lawrence Stedman. According to Stedman: "In the 1980s, school critics often exaggerated the size and extent of the test score decline. In spite of enormous changes in society and school populations, U.S. achievement has been remarkably stable for many decades. But it remains inadequate and at low levels."[124]

The argument here is simple. There is almost certainly a crisis in American education. It is a crisis that has been going on for at least 100 years. As argued elsewhere in this work, the consensus Hirsch and others assume that has existed in the past is a myth. Schools need to be improved, but not to return to the standards of an earlier era.

## Hirsch's Desire for a National Curriculum

To a large extent, Hirsch, in his efforts as an educational reformer, wants to establish a national curriculum.

> Our elementary schools are not only dominated by the content-neutral ideas of Rousseau and Dewey, they are also governed by approximately sixteen thousand independent school districts. We have viewed this dispersion of educational authority as an insurmountable obstacle to altering the fragmentation of the school curriculum even when we have questioned that fragmentation. We have permitted school policies that have shrunk the body of information that

> Americans share and these policies have caused our national literacy to decline.[125]

This is an interesting argument when interpreted in a conservative political context. While calling for greater local control, Hirsch and other conservatives call for a curriculum that is controlled not at the state and local level, but at the national level by the federal government.

Putting contradictions like this aside, the question arises as to whether or not Hirsch even has a viable curriculum. In an early review of Hirsch's *Cultural Literacy*, Hazel Whitman Hertzberg criticized the book and its list of 5,000 things every American needs to know for its fragmentation. As she explained:

> Hirsch's remedy for curricular fragmentation looks suspiciously like more fragmentation. Outside of the dubious claim that his list represents what literate people know, there is nothing that holds it together besides its arrangement in alphabetical order. Subject-matter organization is ignored. It is not hard to imagine how Hirsch's proposal would have been greeted by educational neoconservatives had it been made by one of those professors of education who he charges are responsible for the current state of cultural illiteracy.[126]

Hertzberg wonders what Hirsch's "hodgepodge of miscellaneous, arbitrary, and often trivial information" would look like if it were put into a coherent curriculum.

In 1988 Hirsch did in fact establish the Core Knowledge Foundation, which had as its purpose the design of a national curriculum. Called the "Core Knowledge Sequence," the sequence offered a curriculum in six content areas: history, geography, mathematics, science, language arts, and fine arts. Hirsch's curriculum was intended to represent approximately half of the total curriculum for K-6 schools. Subsequent curriculum revisions include a curriculum for grades seven and eight as well as one at the preschool level.[127]

Several hundred schools across the United States currently use Hirsch's model. A national conference is held each year, which draws several thousand people. In books like *What Your First Grader Needs to Know* (1991) as well *A First Dictionary of Cultural Literacy: What Our Children Need to Know* (1989) and

*The Dictionary of Cultural Literacy* (1993), along with the Core Knowledge Sequence, one finds a fairly conservative but generally useful curriculum that conforms to much of the content already found in local school systems around the country.

Hirsch seems not to recognize that there indeed is a national curriculum, one whose standards are set by local communities through their acceptance and rejection of textbooks and by national accreditation groups ranging from the National Council of Teachers of Mathematics to the National Council for Social Studies Teachers and the National Council of Teachers of English. One need only look at standards in different subject areas in school districts across the country to realize the extent to which there is indeed a national curriculum.

Whether the current curriculum in use in the schools across the country is adequate is of course open to debate. Creating any curriculum is by definition a deeply political act, and is, or should be, subject to considerable negotiation and discussion at any level. But to act as though there is not a de facto national curriculum is simply inaccurate. First graders in most school districts across the country learn about the weather and the seasons, along with more basic skills like adding and subtracting. Students do not learn to divide before they learn how to add or multiply. Local and state history is almost universally introduced for the first time in either third or fourth grade. It is reintroduced in most states at the seventh or eighth grade levels. Algebra is typically taught in the ninth grade. Traditions, developmental patterns of students, textbook content, and national subject standards combine to create a fairly uniform national curriculum.

Hirsch's complaint that there is no national curriculum is not motivated by a desire to establish one but rather a desire to establish a curriculum that reflects his cultural and ideological orientation. It is a sophisticated assault on more inclusive and diverse models of curriculum and culture—one that represents a major battle in the culture wars of the last twenty years in the United States.

## Who Creates and Defines the Curriculum?

The questions of who creates and controls the curriculum and what its content should be are open to constant debate, negotiation, and modification in any culture. I wish to argue for a broader conception of culture and curriculum than that put forward by Hirsch and other conservative cultural critics. The American experience is one that is owned by its entire people. The experience of slavery, the oppression of gays, the conquest of Native Americans, and the fight for the rights of women are part of the history of every American citizen, as well as the stories of the victors and winners in our social, economic, and political system Hirsch so strongly favors.

We as a people need to expand our vision of America and its culture beyond the narrow elitism of Hirsch and other cultural conservatives. At the same time, the isolationism and political correctness of discriminated against and overlooked groups needs to be overcome.

How then is a common ground established in our culture? First, it is achieved through an understanding broader than that suggested by Hirsch and his list of 5,000 things every American needs to know. Lists like Hirsch's may be more helpful for what they exclude than for what they include. In the case of this book, by proposing an alternative cultural list for literate Americans—a list of what "every American ought to know"—we can begin to engage in a dialogue over which knowledge is in fact most important to us as a culture and a people. Perhaps in the end what is important is not simply the knowledge implied by Hirsch's list, or my own list, or anyone else's list, but how the content of each list can be used as a starting point for discussion, exchanges, and creating a world in which there is greater mutual understanding.

Alternative lists of the type that I have put forward also suggest the possibility of a greater critical consciousness and engagement. The words that make up the list at the end of this book are, as compared to Hirsch's, arguably more provocative, more probing, and often "darker." They are intended to provoke dialogue, engagement, and critical thinking, rather than simply acceptance. They are deliberately designed to fly in the face of

Hirsch's overly simplified and naive "transmission model" of culture and learning.

Facts and information are important to learning. They provide essential building blocks for both children and adults to construct interpretation and meaning—ones that ultimately help them to identify what Bateson describes as the "pattern which connects." Although Hirsch provides the learner with an interesting set of building blocks or units for the construction of culture, he does not make clear that they are not the only set of blocks or units that can be used. At the same time, he fails to show the possibility that concepts can be built in other ways than his rather strict and limited models prescribe.

In addition, Hirsch has very little idea that his "constructions of culture" are deeply rooted in a fairly narrow, limited, and self-serving perspective. Hirsch has little idea of this country's complexity and diversity. He is someone who hides under a liberal/democratic veneer, but who is in fact, from the evidence found in his writing, an authoritarian and conservative thinker and reformer. He has constructed a selective and self-serving model of culture and education—one that often seems naive, or at the very best poorly researched and thought through.

For example, as pointed out so effectively by Donaldo Macedo in his book *Literacies of Power: What Americans Are Not Allowed to Know*, Hirsch's descriptions of historical events in works like his *Dictionary of Cultural Literacy: What Every American Needs to Know* (a direct outgrowth of his book *Cultural Literacy*) are highly selective. His description of the Navahos, for example, is as follows:

> **Navahos:** A tribe of Native Americans, the most numerous in the United States. The Navahos have reservations in the Southwest.
>
> The Navahos were forced to move by the United States troop under Kit Carson in 1864. They call the march, on which many died, the Long Walk.
>
> Today, they are known for their houses, called hogans, made of logs and earth; for their work as ranchers and shepherds; and for their skill in producing blankets and turquoise and silver jewelry.[128]

Macedo, drawing on the work of Noam Chomsky, talks about the "resettlement" of the Navahos in the context of the destruction and conquest of native population as part of the European settlement. He cites figures to the effect that 12 to 15 million people lived north of the Rio Grande prior to the European settlement, compared to 200,000 by the year 1900. Hirsch overlooks critical social issues of genocide and conquest affecting the Navahos, and instead describes them in terms of their blanket- and jewelry-making. No discussion is included of their being what Joel Spring refers to as a dominated culture— forcibly made part of the "American experience."

The black political activist Rosa Parks is described by Hirsch as:

> A black seamstress from Montgomery, Alabama, who in 1955 refused to give up her seat to a white person, as she was legally required to do. Her mistreatment after refusing to give up her seat led to a boycott of the Montgomery buses by supporters of equal rights for black people. The incident was the first major confrontation in the Civil Rights Movement.[129]

Although on the surface, Hirsch's description seems like a simple telling of the facts, it distorts by its omissions and oversimplifications. Rosa Parks, for example, was not simply a seamstress but a political activist who had actively worked for years as a leader of the local National Association for the Advancement of Colored People. She was trained in non-confrontational methods at the Highlander Folk School. And, as Macedo has pointed out, she was not simply "mistreated," but arrested and placed in jail as a result of her actions.[130]

The selective interpretation of cultural material conducted by Hirsch is compounded by the failure to include certain materials or only barely include them. In *The Dictionary of Cultural Literacy*, for example, slavery and the slave trade are limited to the following entry:

> **Slave trade** The transportation of slaves from Africa to North and South America between the seventeenth and nineteenth century. Congress banned the importing of slaves into the United States in 1808.[131]

This is in a book numbering more than 600 pages, where the entry on the "Organization of Petroleum Exporting Countries" (OPEC) is three times as long,[132] and the entry for the word "paradox" twice as long as that for the slave trade.[133]

Hirsch's interpretation of the essentials of American culture, as demonstrated above, is further complicated by what those essentials even mean. His monocultural approach ignores the reality that the United States represents a multiplicity of cultures, each with its own social, political, and cultural claims. Often the goals of these groups, from African Americans to Afro-Caribbeans to Latinos, gays, lesbians, and feminists, to name just a few, are markedly different from one another. As Todd Gitlin points out, "these groups are often in competition and contentious with one another ... all feel they have been silent too long while their people suffer. The result is a cacophony without much listening or the sympathy needed to keep up a common conversation."[134]

Hirsch's desire for common cultural core is not only naive but distorts the American historical experience. As Todd Gitlin has pointed out, there is a mythology about American culture and society in which there existed in a not-too-distant past a cultural consensus "about the virtue of Western civilization, the nature of merit and authority, the rules of reason, the proper constitution of canon and curriculum, the integrity of American history, the civility of men."[135] As Gitlin makes clear in his book *The Twilight of Common Dreams*, the United States, unlike other cultures, has not so much had a clear vision of what it means to be an American, but instead has had a tradition of "dreaming" about the possibilities of a future.

## Why Is Hirsch's Work So Readily Accepted?

Richard Ognibene, in a 1998 article titled "Social Foundations and School Reform Networks," argues that many of the reviewers of Hirsch's *The Schools We Need* displayed little critical insight, and in fact many of their reviews may have been driven by their own ideological points of view. Ognibene, for example, quotes a 1997 *Commentary* review to the effect that Hirsch's book was a "a tour de force ... a compact and lucid history of American thought during the past century... that argues convincingly that the implementation of progressive educational ideas has actually served to deepen the very class stratification the Progressives originally sought to combat."[136] An October 1996 review of Hirsch's *The Schools We Need* is described by Albert Shanker, the president of the American Federation of Teachers, as a "brilliant, combative, and intensely practical discussion of how our educational system got into its current mess and what we must do to pull it out."[137] Ognibene comments that:

> Students might be puzzled about why the President of the American Federation of Teachers, probably the best known educator of his time, was so supportive of a text whose main message focused on the failure of America's schools. Shanker's analysis was simply another example of a brilliant strategy he had been employing for years, namely, to support reform ideas that deflect any real analysis about how teachers and their unions impede real educational reform. Shanker's general support for higher standards and his specific endorsement of core knowledge costs the union movement nothing and gains support from conservatives and from the general public. This lofty rhetoric covers a business as usual approach that satisfies union needs.[138]

Ognibene extends his analysis by explaining that part of Hirsch's perverse brilliance and success lies in the fact that he absolves the teachers who work in the schools from any responsibility for the problems at work in the educational system. The failure of the educational system lies instead in what Hirsch describes as "the controlling system of ideas that currently prevents needed changes from being contemplated or understood."[139]

As Ognibene suggests, Hirsch's work as an educational reformer fits into important existing cultural and political agendas. This probably explains, in part, its extraordinary success. President George W. Bush, for example, does not have to be particularly interested in the Western canon to find Hirsch's curriculum useful in enacting the "No Child Left Behind" legislation. A relatively fixed curriculum like Hirsch's provides a ideal means by which to establish "standards" on subjects that are considered dangerous such as sex education, evolution, and bilingual education.[140] According to Henry Giroux:

> In this perspective, character is allegedly developed by memorizing dates and facts, on the one hand, while on the other the history of great men overrides any understanding of those struggles waged by labor, feminists, and civil rights movements that have shaped the history of the United States. Critical historical narratives are viewed as dangerous by the Bush administration, as are any pedagogical approaches that encourage teachers and students to become responsible agents actively questioning and negotiating the relationships between theory and practice, critical analysis and common sense, and learning and social change.[141]

In this context, as Giroux points out, the study of a subject like history does not have as its purpose expanding critical awareness, nor to develop a culture of questioning, but instead the rigid acceptance of a narrow vision of patriotism and culture—one typified by the idea of "my country, right or wrong."

## Questions for E. D. Hirsch, Jr., and Other Educational and Cultural Conservatives

I would maintain that there are a large number of questions that educational and cultural conservatives like E. D. Hirsch, Jr., need to answer. In most instances they are questions that have been raised in different contexts by a wide range of critical educational and cultural theorists. They are questions that repeat many of the issues already described in this work, and also challenge Hirsch's assumptions.

*What constitutes really useful knowledge? Whose interest does it serve? What kinds of social relations does it structure and at what price?*[142]

This is among the most fundamental questions that Hirsch and his fellow conservatives fail to address. Hirsch assumes that there is a fundamental core of knowledge that is the foundation of American culture. He believes that this core knowledge is largely self-evident and defines what it is to be an American. As he explains, there is a need for an "anthropological model of education" since

> ... all human communities are founded on specific shared information. Americans are different from Germans, who are in turn different from Japanese, because each group possesses specifically different cultural knowledge. In an anthropological perspective, the basic goal of education in a human community is acculturation, the transmission to children of the specific information shared by the adults of the group or polis.[143]

In a highly diverse and multicultural society such as the United States, it is not enough to assume that there is a set and defined culture that all people know. The tradition of competing groups and the struggle for equal representation in American culture makes it different from many other more traditional or homogenous cultures.

Ask an African American, a Chicano, a lesbian, or any of the other many disenfranchised individuals if a consensus about what it is to be an American has ever "reigned." Ask a successful female corporate leader, lawyer, or university president, whether such a consensus existed. Ask the same question of someone from a minority religion.

The reality is that American culture has been defined as much by conflicts as consensus. We are a nation that was born in revolution and that has rebelled over different interpretations of the culture ranging from the Civil War to the civil rights movement. One of our greatest virtues as a nation has been to engage in dialogue and discussion, as well as compromise.

As a result, it can be argued that the most useful knowledge that educated Americans can have concerns the problems and unresolved issues that we face and the democratic principles on which our nation was founded. Such an approach certainly includes knowing key facts and information, but also emphasizes the idea of learners and citizens being engaged in critical discussions and dialogues about the nature and purpose of a democracy. Examples of questions that need to be addressed in such a model would include: Why have certain groups historically had privileges over others? How has this worked out in terms of race, gender, and ethnicity? How has this contributed to structural inequality in our culture? What problems are evident in our culture as a result of inequality? How can inequality best be addressed?

Asking questions of the type outlined above requires the foundation of fundamental background knowledge—knowledge that allows the individual to understand the "patterns which connect" and the forces that have shaped our history and culture. Thus knowledge of the history of slavery, racial discrimination, and ethnic and gender discrimination would be critical. Hirsch's notion that "a human group must have effective communications to function effectively" is obvious.[144] Such communication is predicated, however, on much more than a common foundation of information or "shared culture."[145] Instead it may be based on the sharing of conflicting and sometimes contradictory models that are discussed, debated, and negotiated. Hirsch, by arguing that "Only by accumulating shared symbols, and the shared information that the symbols represent, can we learn to communicate effectively with one another in our national community"[146] leaves out the critical elements of dialogue and exchange.

Dialogue, discussion, and debate, with a sound foundation in historical facts and truth, have a much greater potential to lead us to the ideals of a democratic culture and society than a transmission model of education that selects what "every educated American needs to know." Hirsch fails to recognize that the American culture may, in fact, be defined by the debate over what our culture is and what it represents.

*What and whose knowledge will be included in a national curriculum?*[147]

In reference to any curriculum, Kristen Buras asks "What and whose knowledge is to be included or excluded? Who will decide?"[148] To a large extent, one's inclusion in the curriculum of any school or culture is a reflection of social and political power. Representation and inclusion does not take place unless one has power. This has been a reality of American history, which can be demonstrated by any careful examination of the experience of groups as diverse as African Americans, women, immigrants, and ethnic minorities. National curricula will exclude their history and specific cultural issues, as a means of maintaining power and the status quo.

*What is literacy? What does it mean to be literate?*

Literacy is defined by Hirsch within a relatively narrow range of traditions and experiences. Despite his declarations to the contrary, Hirsch leaves out much that is essential to alternative views of American culture and society (see the alternative list of 5,000 items "literate Americans ought to know" later in this book.). Historical literacy needs to be much more than the list of the victors. As Todd Gitlin explains, "you don't know American history unless you know the victims as well as the victors."[149]

Cultural literacy and the meaning of what it is to be literate are far more sophisticated and complex than anything put forward by Hirsch. If we are to be culturally literate, we must understand who we are as a people and a nation. Historically we have been a federation of states with significant independence and autonomy. Central control has been relatively weak. Our country was settled by "refugees, adventurers, conquered peoples, and slaves—in sum, by peoples, not by a singular people claiming a common root."[150]

Cultural literacy is defined by knowledge of the complexity and diversity of the American people. It is a literacy refined in the dialogue that is the essence of the democratic process, and that we should pursue as an essential element of education, whether at the K-12 or university level. Such a model assumes that multiple and competing literacies are at work in American culture. These literacies compete with each other for attention and represent an ongoing process of dialogue and exchange. As Henry Giroux and Stanley Aronowitz explain:

> To acknowledge different forms of literacy is not to suggest that they should all be given equal weight. On the contrary, it is to argue that their differences are to be weighed against the capacity they have for enabling people to locate themselves in

their own histories while simultaneously establishing the conditions for them to function as part of a wider democratic culture. This represents a form of literacy that is not merely epistemological, but also deeply political and eminently pedagogical.[151]

According to Giroux and Aronowitz, literacy is political since it is a means by which people can be empowered and disempowered. It is pedagogical because it "always involves social relations in which learning takes place; power legitimates a particular view of the world, and privilege, a specific rendering of knowledge."[152]

*How does school knowledge enable those who have been generally excluded from schools to speak and act with dignity?*[153]

School knowledge that emphasizes a largely transmission model by definition largely precludes the idea of a dialogue and alternative or competing ideas. This does not mean that the knowledge being conveyed is not valid or important. It simply means that it should be subject to *interpretation, contextualization* and *critical interrogation*. Thus Columbus's "discovery of the New World" needs to be critically examined. Whose "New World" was discovered? Was it an "Old World" for the native pre-Columbian populations who occupied North and South American? Was it a discovery, or a conquest, or perhaps even a genocide?

Questions such as those listed above explain in part why in 1992 the 500th anniversary celebration of Columbus's discovery of "the New World" was not particularly well received, as compared to the celebrations held 100 years earlier.

*What are the basics and why are we teaching them?*[154]

The educational philosopher Madeline Grumet makes the interesting point that "If the basics were basic, we imagine, they would be felt in the community. They would be measured in the gait of its people and weighed in the lightness of sorrow."[155] Hirsch assumes that there are basics and they must be taught. In and of itself, this is not a problem. Failing to recognize the fact that there is a selection process involved that "ranks some issues as essential and others as not" is a problem.[156]

One thinks back to the early 1980s and the AIDS epidemic in the United States. Raising questions about and curing the disease was less of an issue when its threat seemed to be limited to the gay community. When the disease began to spread into the general population, all of a sudden its identification and cure became a much more "basic" problem.

Grumet summarizes the issue over the basics in the following way:

> The basics in all their generic and reductive splendor are meaningless to me when promulgated without reference to persons, places, or times. Basic to whom? Basic to what? [157]

These are again some of the fundamental and obvious questions Hirsch fails to answer: What basic core knowledge is being selected? And for what purpose?

*Who speaks in a culture? Whose voice is heard?*[158]

The creation of any cultural canon is by definition selective. Whose history gets chosen is largely a function of power. It is no accident that until the 1960s, women's history and literature were largely ignored in university curricula across the country. As women increasingly gained political and social power, they increasingly were able to change the nature of the canon. As James J. O'Donnell argues: "So whoever 'we' are, our version of western civilization is selective in the extreme."[159]

*How can a democracy be sustained without an ethic of criticism?*[160]

Kristen L. Buras in her review essay of Hirsch's *The Schools We Need and Why We Don't Have Them* asks "how a democracy can be maintained without an ethic of criticism?" She maintains that consensus is essential to Hirsch's theory of schooling. The problem is that consensus—no matter how well-meaning—has the potential to be highly restrictive and undemocratic. Hirsch argues that, "in a large diverse nation, the common school is the only institution available for creating a school-based culture that, like a common language, enables everyone to communicate in a common sphere."[161]

As a result Hirsch argues for the creation of a national curriculum—one he has been implementing since 1986 as part of the Core Knowledge Foundation. The problem with a national curriculum is who decides on the content of the curriculum? Buras, drawing on the work of R. W. Connell, refers to the idea of "curricular justice." What about the possibility of the development of a national curriculum from the perspective of social and cultural groups who have been politically disenfranchised? What if a national curriculum was written from the perspective of race relations, gay rights, women's rights? What would be the meaning and content of a national curriculum from the perspective of Native Americans?[162]

I suspect that such an approach would be inconceivable to Hirsch. Equally, I believe that Hirsch would have great difficulty in understanding the essentially undemocratic nature of his efforts.

*Can there be a shared meaning or commonality in what it means to be an American?*

This is a difficult question. There is a distinct problem in American culture in the way we have lumped everyone together for the convenience of categorizing and naming people. We have "blacks" who are described by their skin color as being the same, while failing to recognize the profound social, cultural, and economic differences between them. What does a working class or poor black woman in her late 50s from rural Georgia have in common with a teenage "black" immigrant male from Somalia? What do "Latinos," including Colombians, Puerto Ricans, Argentineans, Mexicans, and Cubans hold in common? What about communities based on sexual orientation, and so on?

Our diversity as Americans is a reality that binds us together—perhaps as no other single factor. The debate over culture, the dialogue it engenders and requires, is what defines us. Cultural literacy cannot be a static and conservative phenomenon of the type conceived by Hirsch, but instead must be an active and engaged process—one requiring constant reinterpretation and negotiation. We must go beyond our labels and avoid isolating ourselves from one another as we negotiate who and what we are as a people.[163]

Although it would be comforting to tell a single story about the progress and advancement of the American people, the reality is that there is no single story, except that there are many stories, many dialogues, and many outcomes. The United States is a plurality. Its language and culture is far more dynamic and varied than the limited model of cultural literacy put forward by Hirsch and like-minded critics. The anxiety we have about our culture and who we are is understandable. It is also probably inevitable. American culture, with its different religions, languages, geographies, and its commitment to equality and the dream of human perfectibility, cannot be so easily pigeonholed and categorized as Hirsch would like. It is our curse and challenge as a people, our blessing and our future.

\*       \*       \*

There are many other questions that need to be asked in relationship to Hirsch and the contemporary conservative movement in education. Some are new. Many are variations on questions that have already been answered or themes that have been examined in detail in this work:

- What do test scores measure anyway?[164]
- How does one come to self understanding.[165]
- How does one situate oneself in history?[166]
- How does one relate questions of knowledge to power?[167]
- How do we understand the limitations of our institutions, or even of our age?[168]
- Where does the language of those in power come from?[169]
- Whose interests do certain models of instruction promote?[170]

- What are the value assumptions underlying specific models of instruction?[171]
- Can learning take place if in fact it silences the voices of the people it is supposed to teach?
- What do black and other minority children have to give up to become academically successful?[172]
- In what ways do we want to judge tradition? Around what sense of purpose?[173]
- Are schools to uncritically serve and reproduce the existing society or challenge the social order to develop and advance in democratic imperatives?[174]
- How is identity constructed?[175]

Addressing these and many of the other questions raised in this work represents not only a critical interrogation of Hirsch but also of the conservative educational movement in the United States. Following Hirsch, I would agree that "To be culturally literate is to possess the basic information needed to thrive in the modern world."[176] The key issue here, however, is: What is the basic information that we need to know? I believe that this knowledge should be created through a process of sharing, exchange, dialogue, and inquiry. I believe, as Hirsch supposedly claims, that such knowledge is not something that is narrowly confined to the arts, "nor is it confined to one social class."[177]

Unlike Hirsch, however, I believe that his and other conservatives' models of culture are narrowly confined to a highly privileged and self-serving segment of society. Hirsch's model is in many respects un-American. I believe that there is a great deal more for the American people to know than what Hirsch suggests. We as Americans deserve a broader, more inclusive and democratic curriculum than that advocated by Hirsch and his followers. We ought to know and question a great deal more than we do.

Such an approach raises many different questions: How does privilege function in our culture? Who has power? How is it defined? Why? These are questions that often make us uncomfortable, but they are essential.

Finally, we need to recognize that knowledge and culture inevitably represent contested domains. There is no canon of knowledge that is not self-serving. There is no canon of knowledge that does not preclude other important points of view. Instead of embracing a specific cultural canon like Hirsch's, I would argue that instead we need to pursue the knowledge that can only come through dialogue and the process of critical inquiry—one that essentially includes all Americans.

## Notes

[1] E. D. Hirsch, Jr., Joseph Kett, and James Trefil, *The Dictionary of Cultural Literacy,* 2nd ed. (Boston: Houghton Mifflin, 1993), p. ix.
[2] Ibid.
[3] Ibid.
[4] Ibid.
[5] Ibid., p. x.
[6] Ibid., p. xiii.
[7] Ibid., p. 2.
[8] Randall Collins, *The Credential Society* (New York: Academic Press, 1971).
[9] J. W. Meyer. "The Effects of Educational Organizations." In Marshall Meyer and Associates, eds., *Environments and Organizations* (San Francisco: Jossey-Bass, 1977), pp. 78–109.
[10] Caroline Hodges Persell, Sophia Catsambis, and Peter Cookson, Jr. (1992). "Family Background, School type, and College attendance: A Cojoint System of Cultural Capital Transmission." *Journal of Research on Adolescence* 2 (1992): 1–23.
[11] See for example pages viii–ix of Hirsch's *Cultural Literacy*.
[12] Larry Cuban, *How Teachers Taught: Constancy and Change in American Classrooms, 1890–1990* (New York: Teachers College Press, 1993); and Herbert Kliebard, *The Struggle for the American Curriculum, 1893–1958*, 2nd ed. (New York: Routledge, 1995).
[13] Diane Ravitch, *Left Back: A Century of Failed School Reforms* (New York: Simon and Schuster, 2000), p. 121.
[14] See: Laurel N. Tanner, *Dewey's Laboratory School: Lessons for Today* (New York: Teachers College Press, 1997); and Arthur G. Wirth, *John Dewey as Educator: His Design for Work in Education (1894–1904)* (Lanham, MD, University Press of America, 1989).
[15] John Dewey, *My Pedagogic Creed.* Available online at the Pragmatism Cybrary (www.pragmatism.org), originally published in the *Journal of the National Education Association* 18, No. 9 (December 1929): 291–295.
[16] John Dewey, *The School and Society* and *The Child and the Curriculum* (New York: Dover Books, 2001).

[17] Arthur E. Bestor, Jr., "Life Adjustment in Education: A Critique," *American Association of University Professors Bulletin* 38 (1952): 413–441.

[18] Arthur E. Bestor, Jr., *Educational Wastelands: The Retreat from Learning in Our Public Schools* (Urbana: University of Illinois Press, 1953).

[19] Quoted by Ravitch, *Left Back*, p. 345.

[20] Mortimer B. Smith, *And Madly Teach* (Chicago: Henry Regnery, 1949).

[21] Harry J. Fuller, "The Emperor's New Clothes, or *prius dementat*," *Scientific Monthly* 72 (1951): 32–41.

[22] Albert Lynd, *Quackery in the Public Schools* (Boston: Little Brown, 1953).

[23] Raymond C. Callahan, *Education and the Cult of Efficiency* (Chicago: University of Chicago Press, 1962).

[24] See: Herbert Kliebard's *Forging the American Curriculum: Essays in Curriculum History and Theory* (New York: Routledge, 1992); and *The Struggle for the American Curriculum, 1893–1958*, op. cit.

[25] The National Commission on Excellence in Education, *A Nation at Risk: The Imperative for Educational Reform* (Washington, DC: U.S. Department of Education, 1983), op. cit., p. 5.

[26] Ibid, p. 11.

[27] Hirsch, *Cultural Literacy*, p. vii.

[28] Ibid., p. xiv.

[29] Ibid., p. xv.

[30] Ibid., p. xvi.

[31] John Dewey, *Democracy and Education* (New York: The Free Press, 1944), p. 3.

[32] Ibid, p. 3.

[33] Ibid, p. 76.

[34] John Petrovic, "Dewey Is a Philistine and Other Grave Misreadings," *Oxford Review of Education* 24, No. 4 (1998): 513–520.

[35] Ibid.

[36] *Cultural Literacy*, p. xiv.

[37] Ibid.

[38] Ibid., p. 152.

[39] Ibid., p. xv.

[40] Ibid.

[41] Ibid., p. xvi.

[42] Hirsch, *The Schools We Need and Why We Don't Have Them* (New York: Doubleday, 1996), p. 270.

[43] This is actually quoted by Hirsch from Dewey's *Democracy and Education* in a glossary paragraph at the conclusion of *The Schools We Need*, p. 270. It is in this same paragraph that Hirsch refers to the "progressivists" derogatory attitude concerning "transmission" theories of schooling. What is remarkable is that Hirsch does not recognize the contradiction between what he is saying about the "progressivists" and what Dewey actually says.

[44] *Cultural Literacy*, pp. 208–209.

[45] Howard Gardner, "Toward Good Thinking on Essential Questions," *New York Times*, September 11, 1999, p. A15.

[46] Ibid.

[47] See Gerald Graff, *Beyond the Culture Wars: How Teaching the Conflicts Can Revitalize American Education* (New York: W. W. Norton, 1992).

[48] James J. O'Donnell, *Avatars of the Word: From Papyrus to Cyberspace* (Cambridge, MA: Harvard University Press, 1998), p. 119.

[49] Ibid., p. 120.

[50] Donaldo P. Macedo, "A Dialogue: Culture, Language, and Race (Interview with Paulo Freire), *Harvard Educational Review* 3 (Fall 1995): 377–403. Accessed online through ProQuest.

[51] James Treifel, Joseph F. Kett, and E. D. Hirsch, Jr., eds., *The New Dictionary of Cultural Literacy: What Every American Needs to Know* (Boston: Houghton Mifflin, 2002).

[52] Ibid., p. 123.

[53] Ibid., p. 145.

[54] Alfred North Whitehead, *The Aims of Education and Other Essays* (New York: The Free Press, 1957), p. 1.

[55] Ibid.

[56] *Cultural Literacy*, p. xii.

[57] O'Donnell, *Avatars of the Word*, p. 117.

[58] Whitehead, *The Aims of Education*, pp. 6–7.

[59] Ibid, p. 7.

[60] Ibid.

[61] Gregory Bateson, *Mind and Nature: A Necessary Unity* (New York: Bantam Books, 1980), pp. 3–4.

[62] Ibid., p. 8.

[63] Ibid., p. 9.

[64] Ibid.

[65] Paulo Freire, *Pedagogy of the Oppressed* (New York: Herder and Herder, 1970), pp. 47–48.

[66] Stanley Aronowitz and Henry A. Giroux. *Postmodern Education: Politics, Culture, and Social Criticism* (Minneapolis: University of Minnesota Press, 1991), p. 50.

[67] Ibid.

[68] Paul E. Willis, *Learning To Labor: How Working Class Kids Get Working Class Jobs* (New York, Columbia University Press, 1981).

[69] Henry Giroux, *Disturbing Pleasures: Learning Popular Culture* (New York: Routledge, 1994), pp. ix–x.

[70] Ibid, p. x.

[71] Ibid.

[72] Kincheloe and Steinberg, *Changing Multiculturalism*, p. 51. Although Hirsch declares himself a "political liberal and an educational conservative," he borders on sophistry in explaining that as a political liberal and educational conservative he is in reality "an educational pragmatist" (*Cultural Literacy*, p. 6). He then goes on to argue that "political liberals really ought to oppose progressive educational ideas because they have led to practical failure and greater social inequity." According to him, "The only practical way to achieve liberalism's aim of greater social justice is to pursue conservative educational policies" (ibid., p. 6).

[73] Martin Carnoy, *Education as Cultural Imperialism* (New York: David McKay Company, 1974), p. 3.

[74] Ibid.

[75] John Willinsky, *Learning to Divide the World: Education at Empire's End* (Minneapolis: University of Minnesota Press, 1998) and Linda Tuhuwai Smith, *Decolonizing Methodologies: Research and Indigenous Peoples* (London: Zed Books, 1999).

[76] Carnoy, *Cultural Imperialism,* p. 3.

[77] Ibid.

[78] Smith, *Decolonizing Methodologies*, p. 4.

[79] Kincheloe and Steinberg, *Changing Multiculturalism*, p. 85.

[80] Hirsch, *The Schools We Need*, p. 18.

[81] Gail P. Kelly and Phillip Altbach, *Education and Colonialism* (New York: Longman, 1978), p. 2.

[82] See the bibliography of this book for the works of these authors.

[83] Kelly and Altbach, op. cit., pp. 1–44.

[84] Hirsch, *Cultural Literacy*, p. xiii.

[85] Ibid., p. xvii.

[86] Barry Burker, "Antonio Gramsci, Encyclopedia of Informal Education," available at http://www.infed.org/hp-education.

[87] Peter McLaren, *Life in schools: An Introduction to Critical Pedagogy in the Foundations of Education,* 3d ed. (New York: Longman, 1998),

pp. 177–178. Todd Gitlin defines hegemony as "a ruling class's (or alliance's) domination of subordinate classes and groups through the elaboration and penetration of ideology (ideas and assumptions) into their common sense and everyday practice; it is the systematic (but not necessarily or even usually deliberate) engineering of mass consent to the established order. No hard and fast line can be drawn between the mechanisms of hegemony and the mechanisms of coercion. . . . In any given society, hegemony and coercion are interwoven" (Todd Gitlin, *The Whole World is Watching: Mass Media in the Making and Unmaking of the New Left* [Berkeley: University of California Press, 1980], p. 253).

[88] Quoted by Henry Giroux, *Ideology, Culture, and the Process of Schooling* (Philadelphia: Temple University Press, 1981), p. 23.

[89] See Evan Hadingham, "Ancient Chinese Explorers" available at Nova Online, http://www.pbs.org/wgbh/nova/sultan/explorers.html.

[90] Adam Hochschild, *King Leopold's Ghost—A Story of Greed, Terror, and Heroism in Colonial Africa* (New York: Macmillan, 1998).

[91] Elliott W. Eisner, *The Educational Imagination: On the Design and Evaluation of School Programs*, 3d edition (New York: Macmillan, 1994), p. 103.

[92] Hirsch, *Cultural Literacy*, p. xii.

[93] Ibid.

[94] Henry Giroux, *Stealing Innocence: Corporate Culture's War on Children* (New York: St. Martin's Press, 2000), p. 109.

[95] Hirsch, *The Schools We Need*, p. 7.

[96] Harold Entwhistle, *Antonio Gramsci: Conservative Schooling for Radical Politics* (London: Routledge, 1979).

[97] Quoted by Hirsch, *The Schools We Need*, p. 6.

[98] Antonio Gramsci, "Education." In Q. Hoare and G. Nowell-Smith, eds., *Selections from the Prison Notebooks of Antonio Gramsci* (New York: International Publishers, 1971).

[99] Quoted by Giroux, *Stealing Innocence*, p. 120.

[100] Ibid, p. 117.

[101] Ibid.

[102] Maxine Green, "Review of *Cultural Literacy* by E. D. Hirsch, Jr.," *Teachers College Record* 90, No. 1 (Fall 1988): 149–155.

[103] Stanley Aronowitz and Henry Giroux, "Review of *The Closing of the American Mind* by Alan Bloom and *Cultural Literacy* by E. D. Hirsch, Jr.," *Harvard Educational Review* 58 (1988): 172–194. Reprinted as Chapter Two, "Textual Authority, Culture and the Politics of Literacy," in Aronowitz and Giroux, *Postmodern Education*, pp. 24–57.

[104] Edgar Schuster, "In Pursuit of Cultural Literacy," *Phi Delta Kappan* 70 (1989): 539–542.

[105] Walter Feinberg, "Review of *The Schools We Need* by E. D. Hirsch, Jr.," *Educational Researcher* 26, No. 8 (1997): 27–35. Hirsch's response to this review followed shortly. See E. D. Hirsch, Jr., "Response to Professor Feinberg," *Educational Researcher* (March 1998): 38–39.

[106] Kristin L. Buras, "Questioning Core Assumptions: A Critical Reading of and Response to E. D. Hirsch, Jr.'s *The Schools We Need and Why We Don't Have Them*," *Harvard Educational Review* 69, No. 1 (Spring 1999): 67–93.

[107] Richard Ognibene, "Social Foundations and School Reform Networks: The Case of E. D. Hirsch, Jr.," *Educational Foundations* 12, No. 4 (Fall 1998): 5–27.

[108] Stanley Aronowitz and Henry A. Giroux. *Postmodern Education: Politics, Culture, and Social Criticism* (Minneapolis: University of Minnesota Press, 1991), p. 45.

[109] Hirsch, *Cultural Literacy*, p. 110.

[110] Quoted from Bestor by Hirsch in *The Schools We Need*, p. 63.

[111] Quoted by Hirsch in *The Schools We Need*, p. 64.

[112] Hirsch, *The Schools We Need*, pp. 63–64.

[113] Buras, op. cit., p. 73.

[114] Quoted from Bestor by Hirsch in *The Schools We Need*, p. 65.

[115] Hirsch, *The Schools We Need,* p. 65.

[116] Michael Presley, "We Still Know Little about the Schools that E. D. Hirsch, Jr., Believes We Need," *Issues in Education* 3, No. 1 (1997): 135–151. According to Presley, while reading Hirsch's *The Schools We Need,* he could find little evidence that "convinced me that I was reading an author who has spent much time in American elementary schools or even in schools he might view favorably, such as those adopting his approach to elementary education."

[117] Ibid.

[118] Ibid.

[119] Hirsch, "Response to Professor Feinberg," op. cit., p. 38. See Walter Feinberg, "Educational Manifestoes and the New Fundamentalism," *Educational Researcher* 26, No. 8: 27–35.

[120] Ibid, p. 39.

[121] Ibid.

[122] Hirsch, *The Schools We Need*, p. 1.

[123] David Berliner and Bruce Biddle, *The Manufactured Crisis: Myths, Fraud, and the Attack on America's Public Schools* (Reading, MA: Addison-Wesley, 1995), p. 4.

[124] Lawrence Stedman, "The Achievement Crisis Is Real: A Review of the Manufactured Crisis," *Education Policy Analysis Archives* 4, No. 1, (1996), available online at: http://epaa.asu.edu/epaa/v4n1.html.

[125] Hirsch, *Cultural Literacy*, p. 18.

[126] Hazel Whitman Hertzberg, "Review of *Cultural Literacy: What Every American Needs to Know*," *Teachers College Record* 90, No. 1 (Fall 1988): 146.

[127] Core Knowledge Foundation, *Core Knowledge Sequence (Revised 1995): Content Guide for Grades K-6* (Charlottesville, VA: Core Knowledge Foundation, 1995).

[128] Quoted by Donaldo Macedo in *Literacies of Power: What Americans Are Not Allowed to Know* (Boulder, CO: Westview Press, 1996), p. 71.

[129] Quoted by Macedo, ibid., p. 75.

[130] Ibid, p. 75.

[131] Hirsch, et al., *Dictionary of Cultural Literacy*, p. 264.

[132] Ibid, p. 450.

[133] Ibid, p. 152.

[134] Gitlin, *The Twilight of Common Dreams*, p. 35.

[135] Ibid., Gitlin, p. 1.

[136] Quoted by Ognibene, op. cit. p. 12.

[137] Ibid., p. 12.

[138] Ibid., pp. 12–13.

[139] Ognibene, op. cit., quoting Hirsch, p. 13.

[140] Henry Giroux, *The Abandoned Generation: Democracy Beyond the Culture of Fear* (New York: Palgrave, 2003), p. 91.

[141] Ibid.

[142] Henry Giroux, *Living Dangerously: Multiculturalism and the Politics of Difference* (New York: Peter Lang, 1993), p. 16.

[143] Hirsch, *Cultural Literacy*, xv–xvi.

[144] Ibid, p. xvii.

[145] Ibid.

[146] Ibid.

[147] Buras, op. cit., p. 85.

[148] Ibid.

[149] Gitlin, *The Twilight of Common Dreams*, p. 40.

[150] Ibid, p. 45.

[151] Aronowitz and Giroux. *Postmodern Education*, p. 51.

[152] Ibid., p. 51.

[153] Giroux, *Living Dangerously*, p. 16.

[154] Kincheloe and Steinberg, *Thirteen Questions*, p. 13.

[155] Madeline Grumet, "The Curriculum: What Are the Basics and Why Are We Teaching Them?" In Joe L. Kincheloe and Shirley R. Steinberg, *Thirteen Questions: Reframing Education's Conversation* (New York: Peter Lang, 1995), p. 15.

[156] Ibid, p. 15.

[157] Ibid, p. 16.

[158] Giroux, *Border Crossing*, p. 26.

[159] James J. O'Donnell, *Avatars of the Word*, p. 107.

[160] Buras, op. cit., p. 85.

[161] Hirsch, *The Schools We Need*, p. 233.

[162] Buras, op. cit., p. 87.

[163] Gitlin, *The Twilight of Common Dreams*, p. 35.

[164] Giroux, *Border Crossing*, p. 12.

[165] Ibid.

[166] Ibid.

[167] Ibid.

[168] Ibid.

[169] Ibid, p. 14.

[170] Ibid.

[171] Ibid.

[172] Ibid., p. 16.

[173] Ibid., p. 18.

[174] Ibid.

[175] Ibid., p. 12.

[176] Hirsch, *Critical Literacy*, p. xiii.

[177] Ibid.

# WHAT LITERATE AMERICANS OUGHT TO KNOW— A PRELIMINARY LIST

"When I use a word," Humpty Dumpty said in a rather scornful tone, "it means just what I choose it to mean—neither more or less." "The question is," said Alice, "whether you can make words mean so many different things." "The question is," said Humpty Dumpty, "which is to be the master—that's all."

—Lewis Carroll, *Through the Looking Glass*

The following list is intended as a response to E. D. Hirsch, Jr., Joseph Kett, and James Trefil's list of 5,000 items, "What Literate Americans Know: A Preliminary List," included at the conclusion of *Cultural Literacy*. A similar list of several hundred items was included by Rick Simonson and Scott Walker under the title "Opening the American Mind" in *The Graywolf Annual Five: Multicultural Literacy* (Saint Paul, MN: Graywolf Press, 1988). Many of the items included by Simonson and Walker are also included in the list that follows. This list, unlike Hirsch et. al.'s list, is not intended as a definitive or canonical list, but is intended instead to suggest the limitations and narrow cultural, social, and political perspective of Hirsch's list. I hope it provides a starting point for dialogue and discussion and encourages the creation of competing lists or supplements that can expand our understanding of the meaning of cultural literacy. Those interested are encouraged to submit new words and their definitions to the website for this book at http://www.paradigmpublishers.com/book/critical_literacy.

9/11
*2001: A Space Odyssey*
   (1968)
Abbey Theatre
Abbott, Bernice
Abbott and Costello
Abernathy, Ralph D.
AbFab (absolutely fabulous)
Ableism
ABMs (anti-ballistic missiles)
Aboriginal art
Aborigines
Abortion clinic violence
Abraham Lincoln Brigade
Abstract
Abstract expressionism
Absurd
Absurd, theater of the
Abu-Jamal, Mumia
Abzug, Bella
Accessed voices
Ache
Achebe, Chinua
Acidfreak
Acidhead
Acid house
Acid jazz
Acid pad
Acid test
Acmeism
Acrylic
Action figure
Action painting
Action research
Active aging
Active birth
Active citizen
Active listening
Acton, Lord
Actor's Studio
ACT-UP
Acuff, Roy
Acupressure

Acyclovir
Ada
Ada, Countess of Lovelace
*Adair v. United States* (1908)
Ad creep
Adams, Scott
Adaptable cars
Adaptive technology
Addams, Douglas
Addams Family
Adderley, Cannonball
Addis Ababa
Additive
Adidas
Adinkra cloth
Adire cloth
Adler, Larry
Adlerian
Adobe
Adobe Corporation
Adorno, Theodor
Ad valorem tax
Advanced Research Projects
   Agency (ARPA)
Advertising
Advertorial
*Advocate, The*
Aeneas
Aerosmith
Affluential
Affluenza
Afghan Rebels
Afghan War
African American
African American vernacular
   English
African diaspora
African National Congress
   (ANC)
African nationalism
Afro
Afrocentric curricula
Afrocentrism

Afterlife
Agee, James
Ageism
Agent
Agent Mulder
Agent Orange
Agent Scully
Aggregation
Agitprop
Agni
Agnosticism
Agon
Agora
Agrarian radicalism
Agribusiness
Agrotourism
Aid fatigue
Aid for Dependent Children
  (AFDC)
AIDS cocktail
AIDS Quilt
AIDS ride
AIDS walk
Airhead
Airside
Akbar the Great
Aladdin
Alar
Albee, Edward
Alberich
Albers
Albright, Madeleine
Alcázar
Alcohol, Tobacco, and
  Firearms (ATF)
Alcoholics Anonymous (AA)
Alcoholism
Alcott, Bronson
Aldrin, Edwin E.
Alexander's Ragtime Band
Alexandra Palace
Alhambra

*Ally McBeal*
Aliased graphics
Alien abductions
Alimony
Aliterate
Aliteration
All-climax porn
Allen, Paul
Allen, Paula Gunn
Allende, Isabel
Allende, Salvador
Alliance for Progress
Allman Brothers Band
Alpaca
All People's State
Alpha test
Al-Qaeda
Altair 8899 computer
Altamira
Altar girl
Alternative
Alternative medicine
Alternative theatre
Althusser, Louis
Althusserianism
Alt key
Altman, Robert
Alvin Ailey
Alzheimer's disease
Amado, Jorge
Amateur porn
Ambient music
America Online (AOL)
American and Foreign Anti-
  Slavery Society
American Association of
  Retired People (AARP)
American Association of
  University Women
  (AAUW)
*American Dilemma, An*
American Enterprise
  Institute

American Federation of
  Teachers (AFT)
American Friends Service
  Committee (AFSC)
*American Graffiti* (1973)
American Indian Movement
  (AIM)
Americans with Disabilities
  Act (ADA)
America's Attic
Amerindians
Amnesty International
Analog computer
Analysis
Anansi
Anarchism
Anarchist cinema
Anarchist fiction
*Anarchist's Cookbook*
Anasazi
Anaya, Rudolfo
Ancestor worship
Anderson, Marian
Andre the Giant
Androcentric rule
Androcles
Androgyne
Android
Andropause
Angel dust
Angel Island
Angelou, Maya
Angioplasty
Anglo-Irish Agreement
Angry young men
Angst
Aniline dyes
Anima
*Animal Farm* (1945)
*Animal House* (1978)
Animalist
Animal Liberation Front
Animal rights

Animatronics
Animé
Animus
*Annales* historians
Annan, Kofi
Annenberg, Walter
*Annie Hall* (1977)
Anomaly
Anomie
Anonymizer
Anonymous FTP
Anorexia nervosa
Answering machine
Anthrax
Anti-aliasing
Anti-American sentiment
Anti-art
Antibody positive
Anti-Chinese riots
Antichoice
Anticlimax
Anti–gay rights initiatives
Antiglobalization
Antihero
Anti-intellectualism
Antilanguage
Antioch
Antitheater
Antithesis
Antitrust policy
Antivirus
Antiwar movement
Anu
Anubis
Anzaldúa, Gloria
Apache dance
Apache silence
*Apocalypse Now* (1979)
Apocalyptic
Apollinaire, Guillaume
Apollonian culture
Apollo rocket
Apparat

Apple Corporation
Applehead
Apple religion
Applet
Aquaculture
Aquarius
Arab Americans
Arabic
Arabic numerals
Arafat, Yasir
Arbus, Diane
Arcade game
Archaeology of knowledge
Area studies
Arecibo Observatory
Arenas, Reinaldo
Arendt, Hannah
Arias, Oscar Sanchez
Aries, Phillipe
Arkwright, Richard
Armchair general
Armenian genocide
Armory show
Arms race
Armstrong, Neil A.
Aromatherapy
Aronowitz, Stanley
Around the Horn
ARPANet (Advanced
    Research Projects
    Agency Network)
Art deco
Artificial life
Artificial reality
*Art in the Age of Mechanical*
    *Reproduction*
Arts and crafts movement
Artsy
Aryan Nation
Asbestos
ASCII (American Standard
        Code for Information
    Interchange)

Ashanti
Ashbery, John
Ashcan School
Ashram
Ashurbanipal
Asian Exclusion Act
Asoka
Aspen movie map
Aspirin
As seen on TV
Assembly language
Assembly line
Asset
Astarte
Astor, John Jacob
Astroturf
Asynchronous
Atari
Ataturk, Kemal
Atget, Eugene
Atkins, Chet
Atkinson, Ti-Grace
Atlanta University
Atlas, Charles
Atonal music
Attention deficit disorder
    (ADD)
Attention span
Attica
Attucks, Crispus
Atwood, Margaret
Audhumbla
Audioconferencing
Audio Home Recording Act
    (1992)
Audiomining
Audiophile
Augmented intelligence
Augmented reality
Aunt
Auteur
Authentic relations
Authoring language

Authoritarianism
Authority
*Autobiography of Malcolm X*
Autocad
Autodidact
Automated teller machine
        (ATM)
Autonomy
Avant-garde
Avant-garde dance
Avant-garde music
Avatar
Avedon, Richard
Awesome
AWOL (absent without leave)
Axiology
Axis, Sally
Axis of Evil
Ayatollah Khomeini
Azidothymidine
Aztec calendar stone
*Azucar!*

Baba Yar
Babbage, Charles
Babbage disease
Babble
Baby-boomer
Baby-boomer nostalgia
Bacchanalia
Back-channel media
Back door
Backroom Boys
Backstory
Backup
Backward masking
Backwards baseball caps
Bad
Badass
Badlands National Park
Bad-mouth
Baedeker
Baez, Joan

Baggravation
Bag lady
Bag people
Bahai
Baikal, Lake
Bail
Bailey, Pearl (Mae)
Bailout
Baird, Bill and Cora
Baird, Zoë
Baja, California
Bakelite
Baker, Ella Josephine
Bakhtin, Mikhail
Bakunin, Mikhail
Balance of Terror
Balch, Emily Greene
Bald eagle
Balder
Baldwin, James Arthur
Baleen whale
Balfour Declaration
Ball, Lucille
Ballard, J. G.
Ball-bearing hostess
Ballet de Trocadero
Ballet Russe de Monte Carlo
Ballyhoo
Balmaceda, José Manuel
Bambara, Toni Cade
Bamboo Curtain
Band Aid
Bandwidth
Bankable
Bank Street College of
        Education
Bannister, Roger
Baraka, Amiri (LeRoi Jones)
Barbed wire
Barbie art
Barbie doll
Barbie Liberation Organization
Barcelona chair

Bar code
Bardolatry
Bardot, Brigitte
Barebacking
Barlow, John Perry
Barney
Barnumize
Barrio
Barry, Marion S.
Barrymore, Drew
Barth, John
Barthes, Roland
Bartheleme, Donald
Basho
Basquiat, Jean-Michel
Bastiat, Frédéric
Bateson, Gregory
Bathhouse
Batman
Battered woman
Battlefield nuclear weapons
Baud
Baudrillard, Jean
Beach Blanket Bingo
Bear
Bear code
Beardon, Romare
Beat
Beatnik
Beats, The
Beaver, The
Beavis and Butt-Head
Becker, Howard
Beckett, Samuel
Beeper Babies
Beepers
Behavioral engineering
Behaviorism
Behop
Be-in
Bell, Daniel
Belladonna
*Bell Curve, The*

Bellamy, Edward
Bello, Andrés
Bell Rocket Belt
Ben & Jerry's
Benedict
Benetton
Ben-Gurion, David
Benin
Benjamin, Walter
Bennett, William
Berea College
Berk
Berlioz, Hector
Bernard, Jessie
Bernoulli's Principle
Bernstein, Basil
Berry, Chuck
Berry, Mary Frances
Best-used-before date
Betamax
Beta test
Bethune, Mary McLeod
*Beverly Hills 90210*
Bhabha, Homi
Bibliomania
Biennale
Bifrost
Big Apple
Big Bertha
Big Blue
Big Brother
Big C
Big Foot
Big Harry
Big Muddy, The
Bike Messengers
Biker Chic
Biker Chick
Biko, Stephen
Bilhawk
Bilingual education
Bill Haley and the Comets
Bimbo

Binary code
Binary witch
Bindlestiff
Binet, Alfred
Binge drinking
Bin Laden, Osama
Binocular dysphoria
Bioengineered groceries
Bioengineering
Bioinformatics
Biological clock
Biological determinism
Biological mother/father
Biometric identifier
Biomorphic
Biopsy
Bioregional
BIOS
Biosphere
Biotechnology
Bioterrorism
Biowarfare
Birkenstocks
Birmingham bombings
Birmingham school
Bisexual
Bit
Bitch
Black
Black aesthetic
Black-and-tans
Black arts movement
Blackball
Black bloc
Black code
Black consciousness
Black criticism
Black economy
Black Elk
Black feminism
Black Hand, the
Blacklisting
Black Maria

Black Monday
Black Mountain College
Black Muslims
Black Nation
Black nationalism
Black Panther Party
Black Party
Black Power movement
Black rage
Black Tar
Black theater
*Blade*
*Blade Runner* (1982)
Blading
*Blair Witch Project* (1999)
Blake, William
Blamestorming
Blanked
Blaxploitation
Blend
Blended family
Bletch
Bletcherous
Blink ads
Blip
Bloatware
Block, Herb
Blog
Blood brother
Bloody Attica
Bloody Sunday
Bloomer, Amelia
Bloomsbury Group
Blow job
Bluegrass music
Blue Notes
Blues
Bluestocking
Blurbification
Bly, Robert
B movie
Boas, Franz
Boat people

Bobbitt, Lorena
Bob Jones University
Bobo
BoBos
Bodacious
Bodhisattva
Bodice ripper
Bodies
Body
Bodyboarding
Body parts
Body piercing
Body politic
Body scanner
Bodysuit
Body without organs
Boff
Boggling
Bogolanfini cloth
Bogota
Bogus
Bohunk
Boi
Boiler room
Bolivar, Simón
Bollywood
Bolter, J. David
Bomb, the
Bond, Horace Julian
Bondage gear
Bone marrow transplant
Bonhoeffer, Dietrich
Bonk
Bonnard
*Bonnie and Clyde* (1967)
Bono, Sonny
Bonus Army, the
Boogie
Boogie-woogie
Bookchin, Murray
Booker Prize
Bookmark
Boolean algebra

Boolean operator
Boolean search
Boom box
Boomburb
Boomer
Boomsayer
Boot
Bootleg fashion
Bootlegging
Bop
Border crossing
Borders
Borg
Borges, Jorge Luis
Borking
Born again
Born digital
Borscht Belt
Bosnia-Herzegovina
Bossanova
Botanica
Bottled water
Bottom/top
Boudicea
Bouki and Br'er Rabbit
    Stories
Bourdieu, Pierre
Bowers, C. A.
Boy George
*Boys in the Band* (1970)
Boytoy
Bracketing
Bradbury, Ray
Brahma
Brain bucket
Brain fart
Brain scan
Brainstorm
Brainwash
Braithwaite, William Stanley
Branch Davidian cult
Brancusi
Brand, Stewart

Branding
Brass balls
Brassiere
Braudel, Fernand
Brautigan, Richard
*Brave New World* (1932)
*Brazil* (1985)
Breakdancing
*Breakfast at Tiffany's* (1961)
Breaking frame
Breast implants
Brecht, Bertölt
Breeder reactor
Brel, Jacques
Breton, Andre
Brezhnev doctrine
Bricolage
Bricoleur
Bright Cloud Woman
Brilliant
Bro
Broadband
Brodsky, Joseph
Brookings Institution
Brooks, Gwendolyn
*Brownies, The*
Bruno
Bryant, Anita
Bryant, Louise
Bubba
Bubble-gum music
Bubblehead
Bubby
Bchenwald
Buck, Pearl
Buckyballs
Buena Vista Social Club
Buffalo Bob
Buffalo Soldiers
Bulimia nervosa
Bulletin board system (BBS)
Bulosan, Carlos
Bum bag

Bumb (cocaine)
Bumper-sticker nostrums
Bunche, Ralph
Bundling (sexual)
Bundling (software)
Bungee jumping
Bunker, Archie
Bunraku
Buppie
Burka
Burlesque
Burn
Burnout
Burton, Tim
Bush league
Bush, Vannevar
Bushido
Busing
Busker
Bustier
Butch
*Butch Cassidy and the*
   *Sundance Kid* (1969)
Butch/femme
Butler, Judith
Butler, Samuel
Butterfly ballot
Butterfly effect
Buttinsky
Button down
Button man
Buxom
Buyout
Buy the farm
Buzzword
Bypass
Byte

Cabal
Cable television
Cabrera Infante, Guillermo
CAD/CAM
Caesarian section

Caesar's wife
Cage, John
Calalou
Caldecott Award
Calder, Alexander
Call and response
Call forwarding
Calliope
Call waiting
Calvino, Italo
Calypso
Camcorder
Camera obscura
Camera-ready
Campaign for Nuclear
    Disarmament
Campy
Camus, Albert
Candida
Candyass
Canon
Canonicity
Capek, Karel
Capital flight
Capitalist state
Capo
Capote, Truman
Capp, Al
Capra, Frank
Capricorn
Capstan
Capture
Carbon tax
Card
Cardboard box
Cardboard city
Cargo cults
Carjacking
Carmack, John
Carmichael, Stokely
Carnac
Carnival (Bahktin)
Carnival (Rio)

Carny
Carpal tunnel syndrome
Carson, Rachel
Carter, Jimmy, Jr.
*Casablanca* (1942)
Castro clone
Castroism
Castro Street
Castro Street Fair
Casual sex
Catalina Studios
Catastrophe theory
Categorical imperative
Category mistake
Catharsis theory
Cathode
Cato Institute
Cave paintings
CD-ROM
Celebration, Florida
Celebutots
Celibacy
Cellophane
Cell phone
Cellular automata
Cement overcoat
Censorship
Center/decenter
Center for Science in the
            Public Interest
Centers for Disease Control
            (CDC)
Central processing unit (CPU)
Centre for Contemporary
            Cultural Studies
Chad
Chador
*Challenger* disaster
Chaos theory
Chardin, Teilhard de
Charge
Charleston 35, the
Charlie

Chastity
Chat room
Chattering classes
Chavez, César
Checkers speech
Cheesecake
Chelsea
Chelsea cut
Chelsea Hotel
Cheney, Lynne V.
Cheops, Great Pyramid of
Cher
Cherry
Cherry Garcia
Chess
Cheyenne
Chiapas, Mexico
Chicago School
Chicago Seven
Chicana theory
Chichén Itzá (observatory)
Chief executive officer (CEO)
Chief financial officer (CFO)
Chief Joseph
Child abuse
Child-centered education
Children's Television Act
      (1990)
Children's Legal Defense Fund
Childs, Julia
Chin, Frank
China syndrome
*Chinatown* (1974)
China white
Chinese abacus
Chinese New Year
Chinese Progressive
      Association
Chip
Chiphead
Chiropractor
Chisholm, Shirley Anita
Chocolatetown, U.S.A.

Cholera
Chomsky, Noam
Chopin, Kate
Chorus
Christian, Bjorn
Christian Coalition
Christian identity movement
Christian radicalism
Christmax
*Christopher Street* (magazine)
Christy Minstrels
Chronic fatigue syndrome
Chutzpa
Cinco de Mayo
CinemaScope
*Cinéma Vérité*
Cinematic
Cipro
Circean
Circuit party
Cisneros, Sandra
*Citizen Kane* (1941)
Civil Rights Act of 1964
Civil Rights Act of 1968
Civil union
Clapton, Eric
Clarke, Arthur C.
Class
Class bias
Class domination
Class elitism
Classic television
Classical conditioning
Class inequality
Classism
Classist
Class privilege
Clean room
Clear and present danger
Cleaver, Eldridge
Cleaver, Ward and June
Clemente, Roberto
Click

Client
Clifton, Lucille
Climax
Clinton, Bill
Clinton, Hillary Rodham
Clinton's Ditch
Clipper chip
Clique
Clitoridectomy
Clitoris
Clockless worker
Clock time
*Clockwork Orange* (1971)
Clone
Clonish
Closed shop
Closed texts
*Close Encounters of the Third Kind* (1977)
Clothesline Project
Cloudcuckooland
Cobain, Kurt
Cocaine
Cocaine Gulch
Cochise
Cocooning
Cocteau, Jean
Codependency
Code words
Coen brothers
Coetzee, J. M.
Coevolutionary furniture
Coffee bar
Cognitive inferiority
Cohabitation
Cold call
Cold media
Cold Spring Harbor
Cole, Nat King
Colette
Collaborative filtering
Collaboratory
Collage

Collectible
Colonization
Color
Color coding
Colorize
*Color Purple, The*
Color rage
Columbine High School
Columbus egg problem
Combahee River Collective
Combat boots
Comenius
Come out of the closet
Commodification
Commodified culture
Commodity fetishism
Commodores, The
Commoner, Barry
Common gateway interface
Community
Compact disc technology
Compassionate conservatism
Compassion fatigue
Compatibility
Complex family
Compression
Compulsory heterosexuality
CompuSpeak
Computable
Computer aided design (CAD)
Computer Assisted Instruction (CAI)
Computerate
Computer friendly
Computer Generated Images (CGI)
Computer icon
Computerized axial
Computer literacy
Computer music tomography (CMT)
Computers as theaters
Concept cars

Concorde
Concrete art
Concrete music
Concrete operation
Concrete poetry
Conditioning
Condom
Conehead
Confession
Conflict theory
Congress of Racial Equality
    (CORE)
Conner, Bull
Consciencization
Consciousness
Construction
Consumer goods
Consumerism
Consumer terrorism
Consumption of images
Contact languages
Contact zones
Content analysis
Content provider
Contextualism
Contra
Contract with America (1994)
Control freak
Cookie
Cool
Cool media
Cooper, Anna Julia Haywood
Cooperatives
Co-opt
Coover, Robert
Coparenting
Coquette
Core curriculum
Core dump
Cornell, Joseph
Corn Woman
Corporacy
Corporate concierge

Corporate culture
Corporate power
Corporate speech
Corporate state
Corruption
Corsets
Cosby, Bill
*Cosby Show, The*
Cosmo girl
Costello, Elvis
Couch potato
Couch surfing
Counsel cowboy
Counterculture
Counterfactual
Counterhegemony
Countermemory
Counternarratives
*Country of the Blind, The*
Courseware
Cousteau, Jacques-Yves
Covert operation
Cow
Cowabunga
Cowardly Lion
Cowrie shells
Coxey's Army
Coyote (storyteller)
Crack
Crank
Crash
Cray, Seymour
Cray computer
Crazy Horse Monument
Creation/creationism
Credentialism
Credit card
Creole
Crime against humanity
Crips
*Crisis, The*
Crisp
*Criterion, The*

Critical consciousness
Critical inquiry
Critical multiculturalism
Critical pedagogy
Critical race theory
Critical realism
Critical theory
Critical thinking
Crone
Crop circle
Crossbow
Cross-cultural studies
Cross-disciplinary
Cross-dressing
Crossover
Cross-promotion
Cross-trainer
Crumb, Bob
Crunchy
Crusty punk
Cruz, Celia
Cryobank
Cryogenics
Cryoreservation
Cryosurgery
Crypto-racism
Crystal meth
Cuckquean
Cullen, Countee
Cult
Cultural
Cultural Balkanization
Cultural capital
Cultural codes
Cultural ecology
Cultural feminism
Cultural genocide
Cultural lag
Cultural literacy
Cultural marginalia
Cultural memes
Cultural memory
Cultural metaphor

Cultural production
Cultural racism
Cultural relativism
Cultural reproduction
Cultural revolution
Cultural site
Cultural studies
Cultural workers
Culture babes
Culture industries
Culture maker
Culture of narcissism
Culture shock
Cuneiform
Cunningham, Merce
Cunningham Technique
Cuppy
Cursor
CU-See Me
Cuspy
Custom-fit Levis
Cut
Cutting edge
Cut-ups
Cybercafes
Cybergriping
Cyberia
Cyberland
Cybernetics
Cybernetization
Cyberpark
Cyberpiracy
Cyberpunk
Cyber-rape
Cyberscriber
Cybersex
Cyberspace
Cyberspeak
Cybersquatting
Cyberterrorism
Cyberwar
Cyborg
Cyborgian body parts

Cybotage
Cyburban myths
Cycladic art
Cyclotron

Dacron
Dada
Dae Jung, Kim
Daemon
Dago
Dago Red
Dahmer, Jeffrey
Dairy-free
Daisy chain
Daisy cutter bomb
Dalai Lama
Daly, Mary
Damballah
Damien, Father
Dar-Es-Salaam
Darío, Rubén
Dark comedy
*Dartmouth Review*
Darwinism
Darwin's bulldog
Data recorder
Data capture
Data compression
Data harvesting
Date rape
Daughterhood
Daughters of Bilitis
Davenport, Charles
David Letterman's Top Ten
Davis, Angela
Davis, Miles
Dawkins, Richard
Day, Dorothy
Day trading
de Beauvoir, Simone
de Brunhoff, Jean
de Stahl movement
Deadheads

Deafened
Deaf movement
Dear Abby
Death of the author
Deaver Smith, Anna
Debit card
Debord, Guy
Debug
Debunking
Decemberists, The
Decentered subject
Decentralization
Declaration of Sentiments
    (1848)
Decolonization
Decommunize
Deconstruction
Dee Jaying
Deep Blue
Deep ecology
Deepening
Deep six
Deep structure
Deep Throat
Defenestration
Defibrillator
Deflower
Defoliation
Deforestation
Dehumanization
Delinquency
Deluze, Giles
DeMan, Paul
De-militarized zone (DMZ)
Democratization
Demuth, Charles
Demystification
Demythologizing
Dengism
Deniability
Denishawn
Dependence
Depoliticizing of politics

Depo-Provera
Depp, Johnny
Derrida, Jacques
Desaparecido
Deschooling
Description
Desegregation
Deselect
Desertification
Designer jeans
Designer drug
Designer food crops
Designer genes
Desire
Deskill
Desktop
Desktop publishing
Détente
Detox
Detoxification
Detroit race riots (1943, 1967)
Development
Deviance
Device
Devo
Devolution
Dewey Decimal system
Diachronic
Diaghilev, Sergei
*Diagnostic and Statistical
    Manual of Mental
    Disorders* (DSM-IV)
Dialogic imagination
Diana, Princess of Wales
Dianetics
Dianoia
Diaspora
Diasporic cultures
Dichloro-diphenyl-
        trichloroethane
        (DDT)
Dick, Philip K.
Dictatorship of virtue

Diddley, Bo
Diesel dyke
Diet
Difference
Diffusion
Digerati
Diginerd
Digital
Digital audiotape (DAT)
Digital cameras
Digital cash
Digital computer
Digital divide
Digital evolution
Digital phone
Digital photography
Digital theme parks
Digital TV satellite
Digitopian
*Dilbert*
Dildo
Dildonics
DiMaggio, Joe
Dinah Shore Golf Classic
Dinesen, Isak
Dionysian cultures
Dirty bombs
Dis
Disablist
Disciplinary boundaries
Discipline
Disciplines (academic)
Discontinuity in culture
Discourse
Discourse analysis
Discourse of power
Discrimination
Disgustitude
Disinformation
Disneyland
Disneyland Daddy
Disneyworld
Disorient express

Distance learning
Diversity
Divorce rate
Dixieland
Dixieland jazz
Djinn
DNA computers
Dobson, James
Doc Martens
Doctors without Borders
       (Médecins Sans
       Frontières)
Documentary
Docutainment
Dolce é Gabana
Dolly
Domainist
Domain name
Domain wars
Domestic labor
Domestic partner
Domestic violence
Domestication of S&M
Dominant culture
Domination
Domino, Fats
Donaldson, Margaret
Don't Ask, Don't Tell
*Doom*
Doonesbury
Dope
Do-rag
Dorfman, Ariel
Dorothy
Dot-commer
*Do the Right Thing* (1989)
Double helix
Doublespeak
Double standard
Doublethink
Doughnutting
Dove, Rita
Doves and hawks

Down home
Download
Downtime
Down Under
Downward compatibility
Draft registration
Drag
Drag balls
Drag queen
Dr. Dre
Dreadlocks
Dreamcast
Dreck
Dresden
Dress-down Fridays
Dr. Feelgood
Dr. Frankenstein
Drive-by
Driving while Black (DWB)
Dr. J
Dromologue
Dr. Seuss
Dr. Spock
*Dr. Strangelove* (1964)
Drudge Report
Drug test
Druids
Drumming
Dual identity
Dub
Dub poetry
Dude
Dukes, Daisy
Dumb down
Dumping
Dumpster diving
Dunbar, Paul Laurence
Duncan, Isadora
Dungeons and Dragons
DVD
DVI
Dvorak keyboard
Dwarfs

Dweeb
Dworkin, Andrea
DWIM (do what I mean)
Dybbük
Dyke
Dykes on Bikes
Dylan, Bob
Dymaxion
Dynamation
Dynamic systems
Dysfunctional family
Dyson, Esther
Dyson, Michael
Dystopia

*E.T., the Extra-Terrestrial*
    (1982)
Eagle, the
Eagleton, Terry
Eakins, Thomas
Earhart, Amelia
Early bird
Earth First!
Earth friendly
Earwitness
East End
Easter Island
Eastern Star
East Timor
Eastwood, Clint
Eaters' death
E-Bay
Ebola fever
Ebonics
Ebony Express
Eco
Eco, Umberto
Ecobabble
Eco-efficiency
Ecology
E-commerce
Economic elites
Economic imperialism

Economic inequality
Economies of scale
Ecotourism
E-cruitment
Ecstasy
Eddy, Mary Baker
Eddyism
Edsel
Edubabble
Educational colonialism
Educational Testing Service
    (ETS)
Education for critical
    consciousness
Education mortgage
Effeminate
Egosurfing
Eighteen-wheeler
Eisenstein, Sergei
Eisner, Michael
El Salvador
Elastic clause
Electra
Electra complex
Electric guitar
Electrobash
Electronic democracy
Electronic Frontier Foundation
Electronic mail
Electronic man
Electronic music
Electronic numerical Integrator
    (ENIAC)
Electronic panopticon
Electronic paper
Electronic point of sale
Electronic publishing
Electronic text
Electronic trading
Electron microscope
Elegua
Elevator music
Elitism

ELIZA
Ellison, Ralph
E-mail fatigue
Emancipation
Emasculate
Emblaming
Embourgeoisment
Emcore
E-mentor
Emerald City
Emergency contraception (EC)
EMF risk
Emoticons
*Empire's New Clothes*
Empowerment
Empty nester
Enabler
Enchantress
Encryption
Enculturation
Endangered species endism
Endocolonization
Endorphins
Enemies list
Engelbart, Douglas
Enlightenment Project
Eno, Brian
Enron
Enterprise culture
Enterprise zone
Entertainment violence
Entrapment
Entropy
Environment
Environmental causes of
        disease
Environmental impact
        statement
Environmental movement
Episteme
Epistemology
E-print
EPROM chip

Equality
Equal Rights Amendment
        (ERA)
Erdrich, Louise
*Erewhon*
Ergonomic
Erinyes
Eros
Erotic
Erotic passion
Escapement
Eshu
E-signature
Esperanto
Essentialism
Estrada Palma, Tomás
E-tailer
Ethical hacker
Ethical investment
Ethnic studies
Ethnic studies strike
        (San Francisco State,
        1968)
Ethnohistory
Ethnomethodology
Ethnoscapes
E-trade
Eugene the Geep
Euro
Eurobabble
Eurocentric
Eurocentric domination
EuroDisney
Eurojargon
European currency unit
        (ECU)
European Organization for
        Nuclear Research
Eurotrash
Eurythmics
Euthenics
Event horizon
Evers, Medgar Wiley

Everydayathon
E-Vite
E-wallet
Excess of access
Executive Order 9006
Executive salaries
Exocet
Experimental Prototype
        Community of
        Tomorrow (EPCOT)
Expert system
Exploitation
Expressionism
Extended family
Extinction
Extopians
Extreme sports
*Exxon Valdez*
Eyeballs
Eye-phones
Eye-tracing systems

Faaabulous!
Fabian Society
Face time
Facsimile
Factoid
Factory farming
Facts of life
Fag hag
Fairy
Fairy lady
Fall of the Berlin Wall
Fallout
Falwell, Jerry
Family planning
Family values
Family wage
Fanon, Franz
Fantabulous
*Farenheit 451*
*Fargo* (1996)
Farrakhan, Louis

Farsi
*Far Side, The*
Fashionista
Fast, Howard
Fast food
Fast track
Fat acceptance movement
Fatah, al
Fat Boy
Fat cat
Fat-free
Fat Grrls
Fattism
Fatwa
Fax
Fear of success
Fedayeen
Federal Emergency
    Management Agency
    (FEMA)
Federal Theater Project
Federal Writers' Project
Feedback
Feelgood
Felix the Cat
Fellowcraft
Fellow travelers
Female condom
Female ethic
Female eunuch
Female genital mutilation
        (FGM)
*Feminine Mystique* (1963)
Feminization of poverty
Feng shui
Fen-phen
Ferguson, Adam
Ferlinghetti, Lawrence
Ferrero, Pat
Fertility
Fetishization of bitchiness
Feynman, Richard
Fibonacci numbers

Fiber
Fiche
Fierstein, Harvey
Figure engineering
File transfer protocol (FTP)
Film *noir*
Finanscapes
Fingerprint reader
Finlandization
Finlay, Carlos J.
Firemen
Fireside chats
Firewall
First Estate
First Nations
First-person shooters
First wave
Fiscalamity
Fiscal policy
Fiske University
Fisting
Five Civilized Nations
Five-foot library
Fix
Flag burning
Flak
Flake Flashy
Flame
Flame sandwich
Flame war
Flapdoodle
*Flatland*
Flat screen
Flat tax
Flavor of the Month
Fleet Street
Flibbertigibbert
Flight simulator
Flimflam
Flip out
Floozy
FLOTUS
Flow

Flower children
Fluffhead
Fluoridation
Flynt, Larry
Folk
Folk art
Folk culture
Folk literature
Folkways
Folsom Street Fair
Fonda, Jane
Food additive
Food chain
Food irradiation
Food processors
Food stamps
Foof
Football
Footprint
Force
Forced labor
Ford Foundation
Fordham Foundation
Fordism
Foremothers
Formalist
Formal operation
Fornicate
*Forrest Gump* (1994)
FORTRAN
Fortuna
Foucault, Michel
Founding mothers
Four Living Creatures
Four Tops, the
Fourth Estate
Four-year lesbians
Fractal
Fractal equations
Frag
Fragmentation
Frame analysis
Frame of reference

Fran
Frankel's law
Frankenstein foods
Frankfurt School
*Frasier*
Fraser, Nancy
Fraternity hazing
Fredonia
Free-climbing
Freedom of Information Act
(2000)
Freedom rides
Freedom Summer
Free love
Free radical
Free Software Foundation
Free speech movement
Free universities
Free verse
Freeware
Freeze frame
Freire, Paulo
Fremescence
French disease
French kiss
French postcard
Frente Sandinista de
Liberación Nacional
(FSLN)
Frequent flyer
Freudian
Friction-free capitalism
Friedan, Betty
Friendly fire
Friggin'
Fright mail
Frigid
Fringeware
Fritz
Fritz the Cat
Froebel, Frederick
Fromm, Erich
Frontier

Frost Belt
Frozen Zoo
Fructose
Frump
Fruzz
Fuel Cell
Fuentes, Carlos
Fujita-Pearson Scale
Fukuyama, Francis
Fuller, Buckminster
Full Service Network
Funambulist
Fundie
Fungibles
Funicello, Annette
Funk
Funk Brothers
Funny farm
Furbies
Futon
*Futurama*
Future Homemakers of
America (FHA)
*Future Shock*
Futurism
Futz
Fuzzword
Fuzzy Logic

Gaberlunzie
Gabriel, Peter
Gacy, John Wayne
Gadfly
Gaffer
Gaga
Gage, Matilda Joslyn
Gaia
Gaia hypothesis
Galas, Diamanda
*Galaxians*
Gallaudet University
Gameboy
Gandhi solution

Ganesh
Gang of Four
Gangsta
Gangsta rap
Gap, The
Garbage in, garbage out
    (GIGO)
García Lorca, Federico
García Marquéz, Gabriel
Garcia, Jerry
Garden cities
Garfield
Garveyism
Gash
Gass, William
Gas warfare
Gate
Gatekeeping
Gatekeeping theory
Gates, Bill
Gates, Henry Louis, Jr.
Gateway
Gay
Gay Bob
Gay deceivers
Gaye, Marvin
Gay Games
Gay liberation
Gay marriage
Gay plague
Gay politics
Gay street patrols
Gay studies
Gaze
Gdansk Agreement
Geek-speak
Geeksploitation
Geertz, Clifford
Geldof, Bob
Gendered
Gendered genre
Gendered gaze
Gender equity

Gender gap
Genderlect
Gender neutral
Gender signals
Gender stratification
General strike
Generation 9/11
Generation D
Generation N
Generation X
Generation Y
Genericide
Gene splicing
Genet, Jean
Gene therapy
Genetically modified foods
Genetic engineering
Genetic epistemology
Genetic fingerprint
Genetic screening
Genome
*Genre*
Genres
Gentrification
Geopolitics
Geriatrics
Gestält
Gestalt therapy
Get
Get down
Get granular
Get-rich-click
Ghetto
Ghetto blaster
Ghost dance
Gibson, Althea
Gibson, William Ford
Gide, André
Gidget
Gift
Gifts and occupations
Gigabyte
Gigaflop

Gilder, George
Gilgamesh, Epic of
Gilligan, Carol
*Gilligan's Island*
Gilman, Charlotte Perkins
Ginsberg, Allen
Ginsburg, Ruth Bader
Gioconda, La
Giovanni, Nikki
Girdle
Girl on the Red Velvet Swing
Gladys Knight and the Pips
Glasnost
Glass, Philip
Glass ceiling
Gleick, James
Glide path
Glinda the Good Witch
Glitch
Glitterati
Glitzy
Global
Global culture
Globality
Globalization
Global positioning system
    (GPS)
Global village
Global warming
Globitarian
Globophobe
Glork
Gnatbots for learning
Gnome
Go
Goatee
Gobsmacked
Goddess
Godfather
*Godfather, The* (1972)
Godwin, William
Godzilla
Gofer

Goffman, Erving
Go-go
Golden handcuffs
Golden parachute
Goldenberg, Naomi
Golding, William
Goldman, Emma
Gold teeth
Golden Gopher
Golem
Gómez de Avellaneda,
    Gertrudis
Gómez Peña, Guillermo
*Gone with the Wind* (1939)
Gonzalez, Elian
Gonzo
Goober
Goofus
Google
Gook
Goombah
Go postal
Gordon, Flash
Gork
Gormandizer
Gorp
Gorp gobbler
Gospel music
Goth
Gotham
Gould, Chester
Gould, Stephen J.
Goy
Goya foods
Goyische
Graces
*Graduate, The* (1967)
Graffiti
Graham, Katherine
Graham, Martha
Graham, Sylvester
Grammatology
Grammy

Gramsci, Antonio
Grand narratives
Granular
*Grapes of Wrath, The* (1940)
Graphic interchange format
(GIF)
Graphic novel
Graphical user interface (GUI)
Graphing calculators
Grass, Günter
Grassy Knoll
Grateful Dead
Graze
Great Earthquake, the
Great Hunger, the
Great Leap Forward
Great Mother
Great Proletarian Cultural
Revolution
Great Society
Great White Plague
Great White Way
Green
Green Arrow, the
Greenaway, Peter
Green Belt movement
Green-Corn Rebellion
Greene, Maxine
Greening
Greenmail
Green marketing
Green Party/movement
GreenPeace
Greensboro Four
Greenscamming
Greenspeak
Greenwash
Greenwich Village
Greer, Germaine
Grenada
Grey economy
Greymail
Grinder

Griot
Groenig, Matt
Grok
Grotty
Grounded theory
Groupthink
Grunge
G-string
Guarani
Guattari, Félix
*Guernica*
Guerrilla
Guerrilla filmmaking
Guerrilla Girls
Guerrilla marketing
*Guess Who's Coming to
Dinner?* (1967)
Guestage
Guevara, Ernesto "Che"
Guggenheim, Peggy
Guggenheim Museum
Guinier, Lani
Gulf War
Gullah
Gumby
Guppie
*Gutenberg Galaxy, The*
Gutted
Gutter punk
Guttersnipe
Gweep
Gym bunny
Gymnophobia
Gynarchism
Gynecocracy
Gynecology
Gynephobia
Gynocentric
Gynocritics
Gynomorphic

Habermas, Jürgen
Hack

Hacker
Hacker consultants
Hacker ethic
Hackertude
Hadassah
Haida
Haight-Ashbury
Hajj
HAL 9000
Haley, Bill
Hall, Radclyffe
Hall, Stuart
Hamburger Hill
Hamer, Fannie Lou
Hammocking
Hammurabi
Hampshire College
Hampton, Fred
Hand-held computer
Handicapped parking
Hands-on
Hang glider
Hang Ten
Hang-up
Hanky code
Hansberry, Lorraine
Happening
Happy birthday song
Happy hour
Happy meal
Hardball
Hard body
Hardcore
Hard drive
Hard edge
Hard hat
Hardhead
Hard Rock Café
Hardware
Haring, Keith
Harlem Renaissance
Harmon, Jupiter
Harraway, Donna

Harridan
Harrington, Michael
*Harry Potter and the Sorcerer's Stone* (2001)
Haruspication
*Harvard Lampoon*
Harvard Mark I (computer)
Has-been
Hasbians
Hatchet man
Hate crimes
Hate speech
Haul ass
Hausa
Havel, Vaclav
Hawaiian sovereignty
Hawking, Stephen
Hawthorne effect
Hayden, Tom
Haymarket Square riot
Hays Code
Haywire
Haywood, Bill
Headbanger
Head crash
Head hunting
Head-mounted display
Headphones
Head shop
Head trip
Health maintenance organization (HMO)
Heaney, Seamus
Hearst, Patty
Heat-seeking missile
Heaven
Heavy metal
Hedge
Hedges, Elaine
Hefner, Hugh
Hegemonic ideology
Hegemony
Heidegger, Martin

Heinlein, Robert
Heinz 57 varieties
Heliotropism
Hell
Hellman, Lillian
Hello Kitty
He-man language
Hendrix, Jimmy
Hepburn, Audrey
Hepburn, Katharine
Hepcat
Herbal medicine
Herbal therapies
Heritage
Heritage Foundation
Herman, Pee-Wee
Hermaphrodite
Hermeneutic circle
Hermeneutics
Hermod
Heroin
Herriman, George
Herring, Keith
Herstory
Hesse, Hermann
Hestian
Heteroglossia
Heteronormative
Heterosexism
Heuristic
Hewson, Paul (Bono)
Hidalgo, Miguel
Hidden agenda
Hidden curriculum
*Hidden Persuaders, The*
Hierarchy
Higgins, Bernardo
Highbrow
High culture
High-definition TV (HDTV)
Highlander Folk School
Highlander Research and
      Education Center

High mimetic
High resolution
High-stakes testing
High tech
High yellow
Hilfiger, Tommy
Hill, Anita
Hill, Joe
Hill, Lauryn
Himbo
Hine, Lewis
Hip
Hip-hop
Hippie culture
Hipster
Hiroshige
Historical revisionism
Historicism
History from below
History of childhood
Hit
Hitchcock ending
HIV-positive
Hive mind
Hmong
Ho
*Hobbit, The* (1937)
Hobo
Hobson's choice
Ho Chi Minh Trail
Hockney, David
Hodoo
Hoffman, Abbie
Hog
Hokum
Holiday, Billie
Holodeck
Hologram
Holography
Home
Home AIDS testing
Home Box Office
Homeboy

Homebrew
Homebrew Computer Club
Homeland defense
Homelessness
Homemaker
Homeopathy
Home page
Home-school
Home Shopping Network
Homoerotic
Homology
Homophobia
Hong Kong action movies
Hood
Hoodlum
Hooker
hooks, bell
Hoover Institute
Hoovervilles
Hope, Bob
Hopi
Hop'n Johns
Hopper, Grace
Horkheimer, Max
Hormones
Horney, Karen
Horse
Horton, George Moses
Horton, Myles
Horton, Willie
Horus
Hospice
Host
Hostile takeover
Hot button
Hotei
Hotlanta
Hotline
Hot media
Hot pants
Hot-seating
Houri
House husband

House music
House punk
"House That Ruth Built"
House Un-American Activities
    Committee (HUAC)
Housework
Hovercraft
Howard University
"Howl" (1955)
HTML (hypertext markup
    language)
Huerta, Dolores
Huffing
Hughes, Langston
Human beat box
Human Genome Project
Human guinea pig
Human-machine interface
Human rights
Human Rights Campaign
    (HRC)
*Human Use of Human Beings*
Hundertwasser, Friederich
Hundred Flowers
Hungarian Revolution (1956)
Hunger strikes
Hunk
Hunter-gatherers
Hurry sickness
Hurston, Zora Neale
Hussein, Saddam
Husserl, Edmund
*Hustler*
*Hustler White* (1995)
Hybridity
Hybridization
Hydra
Hydrofoil
Hype
Hyper
HyperCard
Hypermedia
Hyperrationality

Hyperreality
Hyperspace
Hypertext
Hypertext markup language
    (HTML)
Hyphenated Americans

Iatrogenesis
Iatrogenic
Ibogaine
Ice
Ice Cube
Icon
Iconography
Id
Identity
Identity politics
Ideographs
Ideology of domesticity
Ideoscapes
Idiot box
Ife
Iffy
"I Have a Dream"
Illapa
Illiberal education
Ilyich, Ivan
Image
Imaginary museum
IMAX
Imhotep
Immuno
Impecunious
Imperialism
Imperial presidency
Improvisation
In my humble opinion (IMHO)
Incest
Inclusive
Incunabula
Independent
Independent Party
*Index librum prohibortium*

Indian gaming
Indian mutiny
Indiana, Robert
Indie
Indigenous
Indigenous people
Indoctrination
Indonesia
Indoor rock climbing
Indus Valley civilization
Industrial light and magic
Industrial Workers of the
    World (IWW)
Infallibility
Infantilization
Infertility
Infiltration
Infinite Loop
Inflatable scream
Info
Infomercial
Infopreneur
Information
Information age
Information culture
Information storage and
    retrieval
Information superhighway
Information warfare
Infosphere
Infotainment
Infowar
Inkatha
Input
Insider dealing
Insider trading
Instant replay
Institute for Creative
    Technologies
Institute for Policy Studies
Institutional racism
Institutional relations
Intel Corporation

Intelligence amplifier
Intelligence quotient (IQ)
Intensification
Interactive
Interactive computer fiction
Intercontinental ballistic
    missiles (ICBMs)
Interface
Interface metaphors
Internal colonialism
International Brigade
International Business
    Machines (IBM)
International Campaign to Ban
    Landmines (ICBL)
International Monetary Fund
    (IMF)
International Mr. Leather
    (IML)
International Physicians for the
    Prevention of Nuclear
    War
"International, The"
Internet
Internet 2
Internet radio
Internet relay chat (IRC)
Internet service provider (ISP)
Internment camps
Internment of Japanese
    Americans
Intersection of cultures
Intersex
Intertextuality
Intervention
Intifada
Intranet
Inuit
Investigative
Invisible ink
Invisible privilege
Ionesco, Eugene
IQ tests

Iran-Contra scandal
Iranian hostage crisis
Irish renaissance
Irony
Isaacs, Susan
Ishiguro, Kazuo
Ishtar
Isolationism
Isolde
Isometric view
*It's a Wonderful Life* (1946)
Ivories
Ivory Coast
Iztapalapa

Jack
Jacking-in
Jacknapes
Jackson 5, the
Jackson, Janet
Jackson, Jesse Louis
Jackson, Michael
Jacob, Max
Jacquard loom
Jag
Jaggies
Jam
Jambalaya
Jameson, Frederic
Jam session
Jane
Jane Crow
Japanese American
    Citizens League
Japanimation
Java
*Jaws* (1975)
Jazz age
Jazz-rock fusion
Jeep
Jeffers, Robinson
Jencks, Charles
Jeremiad

Jesus freaks
Jet lag
*Jetsons, The*
Jewish American princess
Jewish Defense League
Jewish feminism
Jezebel
Jimmies
Jitterbug
Jive
Jo
Job-sharing
Jobs, Steve
Joe Camel
John
John, Elton
Johns, Jasper
Johnson, James Weldon
John Wayne it
Joint
Joint custody
Joint Photographic
      Experts Group
      (JPEG)
Jolly Green Giant
Jolt Cola
Jones
Jones, Bob
Jones, Chuck
Jones, Quincy
Jonestown suicide
Jook
Joola
Joplin, Janis
Jordan, Barbara
Jordan, June
Joyriding
Joysticks
Juke
Juke box
Juke house
Juku
July 20, 1969 (first moon

landing)
*Jungle, The*
Junk bond
Junk food
Justice
Just war

Kabosh
Kabuki
Kaelin, Kato
Kaffiyeh
Kafkaesque
Kahlo, Frida
Kalahari Desert
Kali
Kama Sutra
Kandinsky, Vassily
Kapor, Mitch
Kaput
Karadzic, Radovan
Karaoke
Karma
Karposi's Sarcoma (KS)
Kay, Alan
Kellogg's Corn Flakes
Kelly, Walt
Ken
Kennedy, Jacqueline
Kennedy, John F. Jr.
Kennedy, Robert F.
Kennedy, Rose
Kennedy, Teddy
Kente cloth
Kepi
Kermit the Frog
Kerouac, Jack
Kesey, Ken
Kevork
Kevorkian, Jack
Keyboard
KGB
Khmer Rouge
Kibbutz

Kibitz
Kick ass
Kidvid
Killing fields
Kilobyte
Kilroy Was Here
Kinderwhore
Kinetic art
King, B. B.
King, Billy Jean
King, Rodney
*King Kong* (1933)
King of Swing, the
*King of the Hill*
Kingston, Maxine Hong
Kinsey report
Kinship
Kiowa
KISS
Kissy-face
Kitchen debate
Kitsch
Kiva
Klee, Paul
Klein, Calvin
Klein, Yves
Klezmer
Kludge
Klutz
Kneecapping
Knee-jerk
Knowledge/power
Koan
Kobo, Abe
Kochiyama, Yuri
Kogawa, Joy
Kohlberg, Lawrence
Kongo cosmogram
Koons, Jeff
Koresh, David
Kosovo
Kozol, Jonathan
Kramden, Alice and Ralph

K-rations
Krazy Kat
Krishna
Krishnamurti
Kroc, Ray
Kropotkin, Prince Peter
Kubris
Kudzu
Kuhn, Thomas
Kundalini yoga
Kundera, Milan
Kung
Kurosawa, Akira
Kvetch
Kwakiutls
Kyoto Treaty

Labanotation
Labeling
Labia
LaBruce, Bruce
Lacan, Ernest
Lacanian mirror
LaClau, Ernesto
Lacoste
Ladies' man
Lagerfeld, Karl
Lagniappe
Lagos
Laksmi
LaLa land
Lamarckism
Lambada
Lambda
Lame
Lamebrain
Landers, Anne
Land ethic
Landfill
Land mines
Landow, George
Land stewardship
Lang, Fritz

Lange, Dorothea
Language as agonistics
Laputa
Lardner, Ring, Jr.
Larson, Gary
Lascaux, Caves of
Laser
Lateral thinking
Latitudinarian
Latrinology
Laughing gas
Laurel, Brenda
Law, Cardinal Bernard
Law of diminishing returns
Lawrence, Jacob
*Lawrence of Arabia* (1962)
Layering
Lead-free
Leading edge
Leading question
Leak
Learning by doing
Learning disability
Leary, Timothy
*Lebensraum*
Lee, Brandon
Lee, Bruce
Lee, Spike
Lee, Stan
Left, the
Legacy
Legacy media
Legal custody
Legionnaires' disease
Legitimate authority
Legitimation
Legitimation crisis
Lego/logo
Legos
Leisure class
Lemon
Lemon law
Leninism

Lennon, John
Leopold, Aldo
Lesbian Avengers
Lesbian continuum
Lesbian feminism
Lesbian/gay/bisexual/trans-
    gendered (LGBT)
Lesbian literature
Lesbian nation
Lesbian studies
Lesbian until graduation
    (LUG)
Lesbigay
Lessing, Doris
"Letter from a Birmingham
    Jail"
Leverage
Levis
Levi-Strauss, Claude
Levittown
Lewinsky, Monica
Lewis, C. S.
Lexis-Nexis
Lezama Lima, José
Liberal feminism
Liberation
Liberation theology
Liberationism
*Liberator, The*
Libertarian Party
Liberty Spikes
Libidinal economy
Lie detector test
Life history
Life of Riley
Life on the screen
Lifestyle
Lifetime learning systems
Lifton, Robert J.
Light-emitting diode (LED)
Lilith
Lilith Fair
Lilith Fair creatures

Limbaugh, Rush
Limited war
Limits to growth
Lin, Maya
Line dancing
Lineal descendant
Linear relation
Linguistic imperialism
Linkage
Link trainer
Linux
Lipchitz, Jacques
Liposuction
Lipstick lesbian
Lip sync
Lipsynka
Liquidation
Liquid crystal display (LCD)
Lisa
Listserv
Literary canon
Little Bighorn National
        Monument
Little Boy
*Little Nemo in Slumberland*
*Little Red Book, The*
Little Richard
Little Rock, Arkansas
Littleton, Colorado
Liveable wage
Livermore Party, the
Livery
Living sampling
Living silicon polymers
Living theater
Living will
Living-room war
Lobbyists
Local area network (LAN)
Lockdown
Lockerbie
Lockup
Locs

Logi bomb
Logical type
Log in
Logocentric
Lolita syndrome
Lollapalooza
Lollygag
Loner
Lone Ranger
Longhair
Long March
Lono
*Looking Backward* (1887)
Loon
Loony-Tunes
Loop
Lorca, Federico García
Lorde, Audre
Lord Greystoke
Lord Haw-Haw
*Lord of the Rings* (1955)
Lords, Traci
Los Alamos
Los Angeles Police
        Department (LAPD)
Los Angeles riots (1972)
Loser
Losingest
Lossity
Lost generation
Lotus-eaters
Loud-seeding
Louisiana Purchase Exposition
        (1904)
Louisville slugger
Lounge lizard
Loupe
Lousy with . . .
Love, Courtney
Love Canal
L'Ouverture, Toussaint
Low-hanging
Low-level munchkin

Lowriders
Loyalty oaths
Lucas, George
Lude
Lukasa
Lula da Silva, Luiz Ignácio
Lump it
Luxemburg, Rosa
*L-Word, The*
Lyme disease
Lynch, David
Lyotard, Francois
Lysergic acid (LSD)

*M Butterfly* (1993)
Mabinogion
Macaronic verse
MacDonald, George
Maceo, Antonio
Machado, Antonio
Macher
Machine gun
Machine-readable
Machinery of representation
Machisma
Machismo
Macintosh
MacKinnon, Catharine
Macoutes, Ton Ton
Macramé
Macro
Macrobiotic
Macrostructures
Mad cow disease
Madeleine
Madelines
Madison Avenue
*Mad Magazine*
Madonna
Madonna studies
Maeness
Maeterlinck
Magic Kingdom

Magic realism
Magnus, Albertus
Magritte, René
Mahabharata
Mainframe computer
Main line
Mainstream
Main street
Major, John
Make
Makeba, Miriam
Makeover
Make waves
Malatesta, Errico
Malcolm X
Male-as-norm
Male dominance
Male gaze
Mall
*Maltese Falcon* (1941)
Malthusianism
Mammy
Managed care
Managerial revolution
Manassa Mauler
Mandamus
Mande
Mandela, Nelson
Mandelbrot, Benoit
*Man in the Grey Flannel Suit*
Mandola
Mandrake
Manga
Manhattan Project
Mankiller, Wilma
*Mano a Mano*
Manson, Charles
Manson, Marilyn
Manufactured biological
    viruses
Mao
Mapplethorpe, Robert
Maquiladora

March on Washington (1963)
Marcuse, Herbert
Marduk
Marginalization
Marginalized academics
Marginalized knowledge
Marginalized students
Margin of error
Marijuana
Marinetti, Filippo
Mario
Maris de Hostos, Eugenio
Markham, Beryl
Marlboro man
Marley, Bob
Marriage
Marshall, Thurgood
Martí, José
Martin, Jane Roland
Martineau, Harriet
Marvel Comics
Marxist feminism
Mary Kay
Masculinist
Masculinity
Maser
*M\*A\*S\*H* (1970)
Maslow's hierarchy of needs
Mason jar
Masque
Mass
Mass (Newtonian)
Massage
Mass consumption
Mass culture
Masses, the
Massification
Mass marketing
Mass society
Mastectomy
Master narratives
Master race
Maternal thinking

Mathabane, Mark
Matricide
Matrilineal
Mattachine Society
Mau-Mau
Maupin, Armistead
Maven
Max
Maxed out
Max Headroom
Maximize
Mayan calendar
McAuliffe, Christa
McCarthy, Eugene
McCarthy, Joseph
McCartney, Paul
McCay, Windsor
McClintock, Barbara
McCullers, Carson
McDonald, Ronald
McDonaldization
McDonald's
McGuffin
McJob
McKay, Claude
McLuhan, Marshall
McMansion
McMillan, Terry
McVey, Timothy
Mead, Margaret
Mean world syndrome
Means, Russell
Meat
Meatball
Meathead
Meat-jail
Mechanistic order
Media Education Foundation
Mediagenic
Media hype
Media imperialism
Media moguls
Mediascapes

Media virus
Mediazation
Medical marijuana
Medium is the message
Mega
Megabyte
Megaflop
Megalithic astronomy
Megalopolis
Megamall
Megaplex
Megastar
Megastore
Megillah
Mekong Delta
Mellow out
*Melrose Place*
Meltdown
Meme
Memling
Memory
Memory palace
Memory sticks
Menarche
Menchu Tum, Rigoberta
Mende
Mendes, Chico
Menendez brothers
Menlo Park
Menopause
Mensch
Men's Health Crisis Network
    (MHCN)
Menstruation
Mental testing
Mentos
Menu
Mercenary soldier
Mercerize
Meredith, James Howard
Meritocracy
Merlin
Meshugana

Mestizo
Meta
Metal detectors
Metallica
Metamorphosis
Metanarratives
Metaphor
Metasearch engine
Methamphetamine
Methodological humility
Metonymy
*Metropolis* (1929)
Miami
Michael, George
Michelson-Morley experiment
Microbrewery
Microcap
Micromanagers
Microniches
Microprocessor
Microrobots
Microsoft
Microwave
Middle Passage
Midgard
MIDI
Midwife
Mighty Morphin Power
    Rangers
Migrant worker
Milarepa
Military-Industrial-Media
    Entertainment Network
    (MIME-NET)
Militias
Milk, Harvey
Milky Way
Millennium bug
Millennium generation
Miller, Lee
Millet, Kate
Million Man March
Milosevic, Slobodan

Mind children
Mind-fuck
Mindset
Miner's safety lamp
Mingus, Charlie
Minh, Ho Chi
Mini-backpacks
Minicomputer
Minidisc
Minimalism
Minimal surfaces
Minimum wage
Miniseries
Minitel
Minoan art
Minor
Minority group
Minsky, Marvin
Minutemen
Minx
*Miracle on 34th Street* (1947)
Miramax
Miranda, Carmen
Mirandize
Mirror site
Mirror writing
Misandronist
Misandry
Miscegenation
Mishima, Yukio
Misogyny
Missile gap
Missionary position
Miss/Mrs./Ms.
Missouri mule
Miss Piggy
Mistral, Gabriela
Mithra
MIT Media Lab
Mitnick, Kevin
Mitterand, François
Mixed marriages
Mladic, Ratko

Mnemonic device
Möbius (band)
Mobius strip
Modem
Modern dance
Modernism
Modernity
Modern primitive
Modigliani, Amadeo
Modular design
Modular programming
Mohammed, Elijah
Mohawk
Mohenjo-Daro
Mojo
Molestation
Momiology
Momism
Monad
Mona Lisa smile
Monetarism
Monitor
Monkey
Monkey Trial, the (1925)
Monoculturalist assimilation
Monoculturalist construction
Monoculturalist power
Monoculture
Monolingual
Monomath
Montgomery bus boycott
Moon, William Least-Heat
Moore, Marianne
Moore, Michael
Moore's Law
Moral Majority
Moravec, Hans
Mordor
Morisseau-Leroy, Félix
Morphadite
Morphine
Morphing
Morris, William

Morris chair
Morrison, Jim
Morrison, Toni
Mortal Kombat
Morton, Jelly Roll
Mosaic
Moses of Her People, the
Mosh pit
Moss, Kate
Motherboard
Motherfucker
Mother Jones
*Mother Jones* (magazine)
Mother's Little Helper
Mother Teresa
Motherwell, Robert
Mothra
Motif
Motown
Mouffe, Chantal
Mount Ida
Mountains of the Moon
Mouse
Movie rides
Mozart
MP3
Mr. Natural
*Mr. Smith Goes to Washington*
        (1939)
Mrs. O'Leary's cow
Mr. Whipple
Ms.
*Ms. Magazine*
Ms. Pacman
Mud, object-oriented (MOO)
Mudge
Muir, John
*Mujahedin*
Mulatto
Multiculturalism
Multilevel marketing
Multilingual
Multimedia

Multinational
Multiple chemical sensitivity
Multiple intelligences
Multitask
Multi-user dungeon or
        dimension (MUD)
Multi-user simulated
        environment (MUSE)
Mummer
Munch, Edvard
Munchausen, Baron von
Munchausen-by-proxy
        syndrome
Munchkin
Muppets
Murasaki, Lady
Murdoch, Rupert
Murphy bed
Muscle
Museology
Museum of Jurassic
        Technology
Music television (MTV)
Mutagens
Mutant
Mutt and Jeff
Mutual-assured destruction
Muybridge, Eadweard
Muzak
MX missile
*My Beautiful Launderette*
        (1986)
My Lai Massacre
Myrdal, Gunnar
*Myst*
Mystery meat
Mythical Man Month
Myth of the vaginal orgasm
Mythopoetic
Mythos

NAACP Legal Defense and
        Education Fund

Nabokov, Vladimir
Naipaul, V. S.
Nairobi
Naive
Naive art (see Primitive art)
NAMBLA
Names Project (AIDS)
Naming
Nancy
Nanny
Nano
Nanosecond
Nanostructure
Nanotechnology
Nanotube
Napier's bones
Napster
Narc
Narcoterrorism
Naronaya, Volya
Narrowcasting
NASCAR Dads
Nation
Nation of Islam
National Association for the
   Advancement of Colored
   People (NAACP)
National curriculum
National Defense Education
   Act (1958)
National Education
   Association (NEA)
*National Enquirer*
National Game, the
*National Lampoon*
National Negro Congress
National Rifle Association
   (NRA)
National Security Agency
   (NSA)
National Urban League
Nattering nabobs of negativism
Natural justice

Navel-ringed rebel
NBC weapons (nuclear,
   biological, and chemical)
NC-17
Nebbish
Nechayev, Sergei
Necklace
Necromancy
Necrophobia
Nectar
Needle exchange programs
Needle park
Need-to-know basis
Negritude
Nehru jacket
Neighborhood
Neill, A. S.
Nellie
Nelson, Ozzie and Harriet
Nelson, Ted
Neocon
Neogeo
Neoimperialism
Neomisogyny
Neo-Nazi
Neoplanet
Neopreppy
Neoracism
Neoscientific racism
Neosocial Darwinism
Nerd
Neruda, Pablo
Netiquette
Netizen
Netscape
Net-wide Index to
   Computerized Archives
Network
Networking
Neural
Neural jacks
Neural network
Neurolinguistic programming

*Neuromancer* (1984)
Neuromantic
Neutrality
Neutron bomb
Nevelson, Louise
New Age
New frontier
New historicism
New lad
New Left
New wave
Newark race riots (1967)
Newbery Award
Newsgroup
Newspeak
Newton, Helmut
Newton, Huey
NeXT
Nez Percé
Niagara movement
Nicad
Niche
Nickelodeon
Nicotine patch
Niebelungenlied
Nielson ratings
Niger River
*Night Trap*
Nike
Nikkei Index
NIMBY (not in my backyard)
Nimrod
Nineveh
Ninja
*Niño, El*
Nintendo
Nintendo thumb
Nirvana
Nitrates
Nitrites
Nitrous oxide
Nixon's trip to China
No Child Left Behind Act

Noah's Arking
Noble experiment
Node
Noguchi, Isamu
Noh plays
Noise
Nonlinear behavior
Nonlinear systems
Nonlinear thinking
Non-neutrality of the
    computer
No-No Boys
Nonsexist
Nonverbal
Normalization
Norplant
North, Oliver
North Sea oil spill
Northern Alliance
Nose candy
Nose-ringed rebel
Novalis
November 22, 1963
November 9, 1989
Nuclear bomb
Nuclear device
Nuclear disarmament
Nuclear family
Nuclear freeze
Nuclear waste
Nuclear weapons
Nuclear winter
Nuke
Null curriculum
Number
Number cruncher
Numeracy
Numerophobia
Nuremberg Laws
Nurturance
Nut
Nyerere, Julius
Nyman, Michael

Oberammergau
Obfuscate
Object-oriented programming
Obliterate
Occidental rationality
Occupational overuse
    syndrome
Occupation of Alcatraz
Oceanus
Ochlochracy
Ochun
O'Connor, Flannery
O'Connor, Sandra Day
Odets, Clifford
Odetta
Off-Broadway
Offenbach, Jacques
Official codes
Official narratives
Offshore
Ogun
O'Hara, Frank
Oikology
Ojibwa
Okada, John
O'Keeffe, Georgia
Okie
Oklahoma City bombing
Okra
Old Blood and Guts
Old Faithful
Old-growth timber
Old Woman
Olecranon
Olive Oyl
Olympic boycott
Olympic Mountains
Olympic Park bombing
Onanism
*One Flew over the Cuckoo's*
    *Nest* (1975)
Online
Online databases

Online press conference
Online soap operas
*On the Beach* (1959)
*On the Road* (1957)
*On the Waterfront* (1954)
Ontology
Open classrooms
Open education
Open texts
Open-source code
Open universities
Operating systems
Operation Desert Storm
Operator
Oppression
Optical character recognition
    (OCR)
Optical scanner
Oralet
Orality
Orbital
Orc
Organ donor
Organ harvesting
Organic
Organization of Petroleum
    Exporting Countries
    (OPEC)
Orientalism
Ortega, Manuel
Orwellian
Oshun
Osiris
Otherness
Otter
Out
Outcault, Richard
Outing
Outlaw technologist
Out of joint
Out of sync
Output
Outsider art

Outsiders
Outsiders' society
Overkill
Overpopulation
Overt curriculum
Ovington, Mary White
Owsley, Augustus
*Oxford English Dictionary*
Oxford movement
Oxygen bars
Ozma of Oz
Ozone
Ozone unfriendly

Paar, Jack
Pachamama
Pacifism
Packer, Vance
Packet
Packet-sniffing
Packet switching
Pack rat
Pacman
Pad
Padilla, Ernesto
Padre Pio
Pagan
Page, Betty
Pagers
Paglia, Camille
Paine, Thomas
Paintball
Paisley, Ian
Paleography
Paleozoology
Palestinian conflict
Palimony
Palmetto slice
Palm pilot
Palo Alto Research Center
        (PARC)
Pan-Africanism
Panama Canal

Panama Canal Treaty
Panama Pacific
        Exposition (1915)
Panethnic
Pangaea
Panhandle
Pankhurst, Emmeline
Pankhurst, Sylvia
Panopticon
PANS
Pantyhose
Papatuanuku
Paperless office
Paper napkins
Paracelsus
Parachute kids
Paradigm
Paradigm shift
Parallel computing
Parallel processor
Pardon
Parenting
Parisologist
Parker, Charlie (Bird)
Parker, Colonel
Parker, Dorothy
Parkinson's disease
Parks, Rosa McCauley
Parlor socialists
Parnell, Charles Stewart
Parse
Parthenogenesis
Participatory budgeting
Participatory democracy
Parting shot
Parton, Dolly
Parts
Party line
Paso Doble
Passive smoking
Password
Patchwork
Paternalistic

Paternal thinking
Paternity
Paterson strike pageant
Patriot missile
Pattern
Pauling, Linus
Pavlovian
Paxophobia
Payola
Pay-per-view television
Paz, Octavio
PCB
PC cards
PCP
Peace
Peace activists
Peace and justice
Peace Corps
Peace dividend
Peale, Norman Vincent
Peckerwood
Peculiar institution
Pedagogical function of
        advertising
Pedagogy as cultural practice
Pedagogy as cultural work
Pedagogy of place
*Pedagogy of the Oppressed*
        (1970)
Pedagogy of whiteness
Pedestrianize
Peláez, Amelia
Peltier, Leonard
Pentagram
*Penthouse*
Pentium chip
People's Temple suicide
Perestroika
Performative practice
Perkmeister
Perón, Eva (Evita)
Peronist
Perot, Ross

Persian Gulf War
Personal communication
        services
Personal computer (PC)
Personal digital assistant
        (PDA)
Personal identification
        number (PIN)
Persons of no account
        (PONAs)
Pervitin
Pesticides
Peter Pan syndrome
Peter principle
Phallocentric
Phantascope
Phenomenology
Phenotype
*Philadelphia* (1993)
Philadelphia Centennial
        Exposition (1876)
Philocalist
Philodespot
Philodox
Philogeant
Philologist
Philomath
Philomythist
Philonoist
Philotherian
Philtrum
Phish
Phoebus
Phone home
Phone phreaks
Phone sex
Photomontage
Photomosaic
Photo op
Photoshop
Phreaking
Phrenology
Phylactery

Phyllomancy
Piaf, Edith
Pica
Pickelhaube
Pidgin
Piece of the action
Piecing
Piercing
Piercing parlor
Pierre et Gilles
Pig
Pig out
Pill, the
Pillhead
Pillion
Pilot
Pilpul
Pimp
Pimpmobile
Pinball
Piñedo, Virgilio
Pinhead
Pink ribbon (breast cancer)
Pink slip
PIN number
Pinochet, Augusto
Pinter, Harold
Pin-up
Pirated
Pirated edition
Pirate radio
Pit bulls
*Plague, The*
Planet friendly
*Planet of the Apes* (1968)
Plangent
Plantation grapevine
Plaskow, Judith
Plastic
Plateau, J. F.
Plath, Sylvia
*Platoon* (1986)
Plausible deniability

*Playboy*
*Playboy of the Western World*
    (1911)
*Plotte*
Plousiocracy
Plug-in
Plumber
Plural identities
Plutomania
Pneumonoultramicroscopisili-
    covolcanoconiosis
Poaching
Pod people
Podunk
Pogo
Pogo (dance)
Pogo stick
Pogs
Point-and-click
Pointy-headed
Poison pill
Pokémon
Polanyi, Michael
Polaris missile
Polaroid camera
Polemology
Political action committee
    (PAC)
Politically correct (PC)
Political prisoner
Politicaster
Politics of representation
Politics of speaking for others
Poll
Pollarchy
Pollock, Jackson
Polyandry
Polygraph
Polygyny
Polymath
Polynesian Ocean Journeys
Polyphasic learning
Polysemy

Polytheism
Pone Bread
Pooper-scooper
Poor People's March on
      Washington (1968)
Pop
Popeye
Poppers
Popular culture
Popular Front for the
      Liberation of
      Palestine
Popular-cultural-commodity
      text
Poro
Port Huron Statement (1962)
Portable
Portals
Portapotties
Porter, Katherine Anne
Porto Allegre
Positive discrimination
Positivist
Posse
*Posse comitatus*
Possibility
Postage stamp
Postcolonial
Post-Fordism
Posthumanism
Postindustrial
Postindustrial society
Posting
Postliterates
Postmodern
Postmodern science
Postracist
Post-Rushdie
Poststructuralism
Post-typographic
Posture
Post-Watergate morality
Pot

Pot libertarianism
Pot, Pol
Potemkin villages
Pothead
Potlatch
Potter, Harry
POTUS
Poulaine
Pound
Pound, Ezra
Powell doctrine
Power
Power bar
Powerbook
Power hungry
Power user
Prague Spring
Praxis
Predatory pricing
Prelapsarian
Premenstrual syndrome (PMS)
Preppy
Pre-Raphaelites
Prescient
Presidential Medal of
      Freedom
Presley, Elvis
Press barons
Pressure groups
Preterist
Preterition
Prima facie
Prime time
Prince Hall
Prince of Humbugs
Prince (the artist)
Princess Alice
Princess Monoke
Princess Zelda
Printed circuit
Prioritize
Prison
Privatization

Privilege
Privileged space
Priviligentsia
Pro
Pro bono
Probability
Problematize
Prochoice
Product placement
Program trading
Progress
Progressive rock
Prohibition
Project
Prole
Prolife
Promo
Prophylactic
Proposition 187
Proposition 209
Prosthetic
Prostitution
Protean
Protean man
Proteus
Prototyping
Proudhon, Pierre-Joseph
Provincial
Provisional Irish Republican
    Army
Proxemics
Prozac
Prude
Pruitt-Igoe housing estate
Psephomancy
Psilocybin mushrooms
Psithurism
Psych
Psyche
*Psycho* (1960)
Psychobabble
Psychodramatic
Ptochocracy

Public domain
Public enemy
Public intellectuals
Public key cryptography
Public radio
Public relations
Pueblo
Pueblo incident
Pueblo Revolt (1680)
Puget Sound
Pulley
*Pulp Fiction* (1994)
Pumped
Pumpkin Papers
Punk
Punk rocker
Pussy
Putting on the Ritz
PVC
Pynchon, Thomas
Pyramus and Thisbe
Pyrex
Pyrrhonist
Pyx

Quaalude
*Quake*
Qualitative
Quality circles
Quantity
Quantum computer
Quantum mechanics
Quark
Queen
Queen Latifah
Queen Liliuokalani
Queer
*Queer as Folk*
Queercore
Queering
Queer Ken
Queer nation
Queer theory

Query string
Quetzalcoatl
Quilt
Quilt knot
Quodlibet
Quomodocunquize
Quotidian
QVC
QWERTY

Ra
Rabbit hole
Race/racism
Racial profiling
Racial slur
Racine
Radical
Radical chic
Radical environmentalism
Radical faeries
Radical feminism
Radical revisionists
Radio talk show hosts
Radio-telescope
Rag
Rage
*Raging Bull* (1980)
Ragnarok, Semiramis
Ragtime
*Raiders of the Lost Ark* (1981)
Rainbow Coalition
Rainbow flag
Rainforest
Rainforest Action Network
Ramadan
Ramanujan, Srinivasa
        Aiyangar
Rambo
Random access
Randomness
Rand School
Range war
Rap (crime)

Rap (music)
Rape
Rapid eye movement (REM)
Rasta
Rat
Rave
Raves
Ray, Man
Ray, Satyajit
Rayon
Reader friendly
Readerly texts
Read-only
Real-audio
Reality check
Reality television
Real time
Real-time information
*Real World, The*
*Rear Window* (1954)
Rebellion
*Rebel without a Cause* (1955)
Reboot
Rebus
Recall vote
Recapitulation theory
Reconstruction
Reconstructionist church
Recycle
Red Brigades
Red Emma (Emma Goldman)
Red Guard Party
Redial
Redneck
Red ribbon (AIDS)
Red Summer (1919)
Redundancy
Reebok
Reed, Ishmael
Reed, John
Reed, Ralph
Reefer
Reet

Reeve, Christopher
Reforestation
Refresh rate
Refusenik
Reggae
Rehnquist, William
Reification
Relativism
Relevance
Religion of technique
*Ren and Stimpy*
Renewable energy
Renoir, Jean
Reparations
Repetitive stress
Representation
Repression
Reprivatizing the public sector
Reproduction
Reproductive rights
Reservation
Resistance
Reskill
Restricted codes
Restructuring
Retail elephant
Retinal scan
Retro
Retrograde
Retro restart
Retrovirus
Reuben (award)
Reverse discrimination
Reverse racists
Revisionists
Revolution
Rexroth, Kenneth
Rhetorical analysis
Rhino Records
Rhizome (biology)
Rhizome (Deluze)
Rhythm & blues (R & B)
Rich, Adrienne

Richie, Lionel
Richter scale
Riefenstahl, Leni
Riff
Rig
Right brain/left brain
Right on
Rights of high school
    students
Rilke, Rainer Maria
Ringer
Ringo
Ring ritual/ring shout
Riot Grrls
Rip off
Ripped
RISC processor
Risk aversion
Risk management
Ritalin
Ritualization of fashion
*Riven*
Roach clip
Road rage
Robertson, Pat
Robinson, Smokey
Robodose
Robotics
Rock and roll
Rock and Roll Hall of Fame
Rock climbing
Rocket book
Rock star iconography
*Rocky* (1976)
*Rocky Horror Picture Show*
    (1975)
Rodman, Dennis
Rodney King Riots
*Roe v. Wade* (1973)
Roentgen, Ray
Rogers, Fred
Rogers, Richard
Rogers, Will

Roller blades
Rolling
*Rolling Stone*
Rolling Stones
Roman abacus
Romance novels
Romantic
Romero, John
*Roots*
Rorty, Richard
*Roseanne*
Rosebud
Rosenquist, Michael
Rosenthal effect
Ross, Diana
Roswell, New Mexico
Rotary piston engine
Rotolacter
Role-playing games (RPGs)
Roy, Arundhati
Ru
RU-486
Rub
Rubber-chicken circuit
Rube
Rubik's Cube
Rucker, Rudy
Rudolph, Eric
Rugg, Harold
Rule of dimensions
Rumi
Run D.M.C.
RuPaul
Rush
Rushdie, Salman
Rust Belt
Ryder, Winona

Sacagawea
Sadat, Anwar
Safe sex
Sage of Concord
Sage of Hannibal

Sage of Monticello
Said, Edward
*Sa-I-gu*
*Sailor Moon*
Sakharov, Andrei Dmitrievich
Salinger, J. D.
Salisbury Plain
Salsa
Samba
Sambo
Samizdat
Sampling
Sampling (music)
Sampling (statistical)
Sanctuary
Sandburg, Carl
Sand Creek
Sande
Sanders, Colonel
Sandinista
Sandoval, Arturo
Sands, Bobby
Sanger, Margaret
Sanitary engineers
Sansei
San Simeon
Santana, Carlos
Santeria
São Paulo
Sapphism
Sartre, Jean Paul
Satellite transmission
Satie, Erik
*Saturday Night Live*
Saturday-night massacre
Saussure, Ferdinand
Sayles, John
Scalable systems
Scalia, Anthony
Scarecrow, the
Scarf
Scarface
Scarification

Scat
Schadenfreude
*Schindler's List* (1993)
Schizoanalysis
Schlafly, Phyllis
Schlemazel
Schlemiel
Schlep
Schlockmeister
Schmaltzy
Schoolmaster of the
    Republic
Schumacher, Ernst
Schwarzenegger, Arnold
Schwarzkopf, Norman
Schwitters, Karl
Science as an engine of
    progress
Scientific management
Scientism
Scientology, church of
Scooters
Scott, Ridley
*Scottsboro* case
Screenagers
Screensaver
Screw
SCUD missile
Sculley, John
Scuzz
Seabrook Nuclear Power
    Station
Seagram Building
Seale, Robert George (Bobby)
Search engine
Search for Extraterrestrial
    Intelligence (SETI)
Search warrant
*Sergeant Pepper's Lonely
    Hearts Club Band*
Seattle general strike (1919)
Seattle Sound
Sechat

Secondary smoke
Secondary virginity
Sedaris, David
Sedgewick, Eve Kosofsky
Seeger, Pete
Sega
*Seinfeld*
Selassie, Haile
Selective perception
Selena
Self-fulfilling prophecies
Selfish gene
Sell through
Selma to Montgomery March
    (1965)
Selma, Alabama
Semi-automatic
Semiology
Semiotic inquiry
Semiotics
Semtex
Sen, Amartya
Sendak, Maurice
Sendero Luminoso
    (Shining Path
    Guerillas)
Seneca Falls Convention
    (1848)
Sensitive
Sequencer
Sequoia
Serapis
Serbia
Serial killer chic
Serial monogamy
Server
*Sesame Street*
Seven deadly sins
Sexaholism
Sex bias
Sex education
Sex equity
Sexist

Sex Pistols
Sex roles
Sex-role stereotyping
Sex-stim
Sex tourism
Sexual harassment
Sexual intercourse
Sexuality
Sexually transmitted disease
      (STD)
Sexual orientation
Sexual politics
Sexual revolution
Sexuated space
Shahn, Ben
Shakers
Shakur, Tupac
Sham
Shaman
Shamus
Shango
Shankar, Ravi
Sharecroppers Union
Shareware
Sharpeville
Shaved heads
Shaw University
Shazam
Sheila
Shepard, Alan B., Jr.
Shepard, Matthew
Sherman, Cindy
Shinto
Shiska
Shiva, Vandana
Shockumentary
Shopaholic
Shopgrifting
Shopping online
Shorthand
Shovelware
Shuttle
Sick building syndrome

Sign
Signature
Silber, Julie
Silent majority
Silicon graphics
Silicon Valley
Silliwood
Silvanus
Simenon
Simpson, Bart
Simpson, Homer
Simpson, Marge
Simpson, Wallis Warfield
*Simpsons, The*
Simulacra
Simulated war
Simulation
Sinclair, Upton
Single parent
Singularity
Sins of commission
Sins of omission
Sinulation
Sirius, R. U.
Sisterhood
Sit-in movement
Sitwell, Edith
Six Degrees of Kevin Bacon
Six Degrees of Separation
Six-Day War
Ska
Skank
Skateboarding
Skatewear
Skinhead
Skinner box
Skinnerian
Skipper
Skirt
Skokie dilemma
Sky-surfing
Slam dance
Slamming

Slam poetry
Slasher
Slave insurrections
Slave narratives
Sleazebag
Slice-and-dice films
Sloane Ranger
Small cap
Smart bomb
Smart drugs
Smart dust
Smashing Pumpkins
Smiley face
Smiling professions
Smith, Bessie
Smoke-free zone
Smokey the Bear
Smurf
Snail darter
Snapping
Snatch
Snoop Doggy Dogg
Snowbird
Snowboarding
Snow White
*Snow White and the Seven
     Dwarfs* (1937)
Snuff film
Snyder, Gary
Soap bubbles
Soap opera
Soca music
Soccer Mom
Social choice
Social class
Social consciousness
Social diversity
Social ecology
Social injustices
Socialist Party
Socialist Sunday schools
Socialization
Socialized medicine

Social justice
Socially conscious foods
Socially responsible investing
Social reproduction
Socioeconomic gatekeepers
Socioeconomic mobility
Socioeconomic status
Sociometrics
Softcore
Solar energy
Solidarity movement
Soma (drug)
Soma (Hindu mythology)
Somalia
Son of Sam
Sonoran Desert
Sontag, Susan
Soul
Soul food
Soul music
*Sound of Music, The* (1965)
Sound-bite
Sousaphone
South Beach
Southern decadence
Southern manifesto
Southern tenant farmers
*South Park*
Soweto, South Africa
*Space Invaders*
Space shuttle
Spacks, Patricia Meyer
Spam
Spam (food)
Spanish Civil War
     (1936–1939)
Spatial representation
Spatial zones
Special forces
Spectacle
Spectroscope
Speech codes
Speech recognition

Speed
Speed bump
Speed dial
Spelman College
Spender
Sperm bank
Spice Girls
Spider
Spider Woman
Spiegelman, Art
Spiel
Spielberg, Steven
Spikes
Spin
Spin Doctor
Spirituals (music)
Splendid Little War, the
Spock, Benjamin
Spoken word
Spooner, Lysander
Spoonerism
Spork
Sportdeath
Spreadsheet
Springsteen, Bruce
Spucatum, Tauri
Squat
Stage dive
Stagflation
Stalin, Joseph
Stalkerazzi
Stallone, Sylvester
Standardized tests
Stanford Research Institute
Stanton, Elizabeth Cady
Star (*) 69
Starbucks
Star of David
Star of Ethiopia
*Star Trek*
*Star Wars* (1977)
Starr, Blaze
Start-up

Stasi
State terror
Stealth
Stealth bomber
Steampunk
Stefano, Joey
Stein, Gertrude
Steinem, Gloria
Steiner schools
Stella, Frank
Stem cells
Stereoscopy
Stereotype
Stern, Howard
Stewart, Martha
Stieglitz, Alfred
*Stijl, de*
Sting
Stockholm Peace Research
    Institute
Stockholm syndrome
Stone, Lucy
Stone, Oliver
Stonehenge
Stonewall riot (1969)
Storyboard
Straight edge
Strait-laced
Strange particles
Strategic Defense Initiative
    (SDI) (aka Star Wars)
Street luge
Strip malls
Structuralism
Structural racism
*Structure of Scientific
    Revolutions, The*
Struggle
Strumpet
Student-faculty sex bans
Student Nonviolent
    Coordinating
    Committee (SNNC)

Students for a Democratic
    Society (SDS)
Studio 54
Stupidification
Subaltern
Subatomic particles
Subculture
Subjectivism
Subjectivity
Subjugated knowledge
Subjugated perspective
Subordination
Substance abuse
Succubus
Sucrose
Suffrage
Sufi
Sugar Baby
Sugar Daddy
Suicide bombings
Suitcase nukes
Suits
Sultan of Swat
Summerhill
Sun Belt
Sundance Film Festival
Super Bowl
Supercomputers
Superman
Super Mario
Supermodels
Superstring theory
Superwoman
Supremes, the
Surf
Surf (Internet)
Surface structure
Surveillance society
Sustainability
Sustainable cities
Sustainable culture
Sutherland, Ivan
Suttee

Suu Kyi, Aung San
Swatch
Swatch time
Sweat lodge
Sweatshop activism
Switch
Swoosh
Sydney Mardi Gras
Sylvania
Symbionese Liberation Army
    (SLA)
Symbol
Symbolic interactionism
Synchronicity
Syncretism
Synergy
Synge, John M.
Syntax
Synthesis
Synthesizer music
Synthetic
System operator (SYSOP)

T-1
T-2
T-3
Tabloid
Tabloidese
Taboo
Tacit knowledge
Tactical
Taft-Hartley law
Tag
Tagalog
Taggin'
Take Back the Night marches
Talaria
*Tales of Anasi*
*Tales of the City*
Taliban
Talkies
Tallith
Tamagotchi

Tammuz
Tan, Amy
Tango
Tank
Tanning, Dorothea
Tantra
Taphephobia
Tarantino, Quentin
Tarantism
Tar-baby
Tarnkappe
Tarot
Tatterdemalion
Tattoo
Tautology
*Taxi Driver* (1976)
Taylor, Frederick Winslow
Taylorism
T-dance
Teach for America
Teaching to the test
Team player
Technical fundamentalism
Technobabble
Technocracy
Technodolts
Technodweebs
Technological determinism
Technology as an engine of
    progress
Technolust
Technopaths
Technophobia
Technopolis
Technorevolution
Technoscapes
Technoshamanism
Technostress
Technoterrorists
Technotwits
Tecumseh
Teflon
Tejano music

Tele
Telecommuting
Teleconferencing
Teledemocracy
Telematics
Telephone hackers
Telepistemology
Telepresence
Teleprompter
Telescam
Teletubbie
Televangelist
Telnet
Telstar
Tenement
Tenochtitlan
Tensigrity sphere
Tenure
Tenzing
Terabyte
Teraflop
Termagant
Terman, Lewis
Terminal
Terminate with extreme
    prejudice
Terraform
Terrell, Mary Church
Territorial imperative
Terrorism
Terrorist states
Terrorists' handbooks
Tesla, Nikola
Testicles
Testing movement
Test tube baby
Tetris
Tex-Mex
Thalidomide
Thanatophobia
Thanatopsis
Tharp, Twyla
Thatcher, Margaret

Thatcheresque
Thatcherite
Thaumatology
Thaumatrope
Theandric
Theanthropism
Theanthropos
Thearchy
Theme park
Theme restaurants
Theory
Theory and practice
Theremin
Theriolater
Thesis
Third Estate
Third wave
Thole
Thomas, Clarence
Thompson, E. P.
Thompson, Hunter
Thonet, Michael
Thought police
Thrash
Three principles of the people
Thrip
Throughput
Thrush
Thule incident
Thurible
Tiananmen Square
Tickle Me Elmo
Timeframe
Time-shift viewing
Tin Lizzie
Tin Man, the
*Titanic* (1997)
Title IX of the Educational
       Amendments Act
       (1972)
Tlingit
Toad licking
Tobey, Twombly

Tokenism
*To Kill a Mockingbird* (1962)
Toklas, Alice B.
Tokyo Rose
Tokyo subway attack
Tolkien, J. R. R.
Tomb of the Unknown Soldier
Tomboy
*Tomb Raider*
Tomecide
Tom of Finland
Tonto
Top-down design
Topology
Topomancy
Toponymics
*Torchsong Trilogy* (1988)
Torino Impact Hazard Scale
Torschlusspanik
Tortoni
Torvalds, Linus
Total institution
Toto
Touch-sensitive displays
Trackball
Trade
Trail of Tears
Tranquility base
Transcendental meditation
Transcultural
Transformative intellectuals
Transformers
Transgendered
Transgenerational
       communication
Transgressions
Transistor
Transmission model of
       teaching
Transparency
Transsexual
Treblinka
Tregetour

Trekkies
Triangulation
Tribe
Trickle-down hip
Trickster
Tricorne
Triggers
Tripp, Linda
Tritheism
Tritram
Trivia
Trojan Horse virus
Troll
Truffaut, François
*Truman Show, The* (1998)
Truth, Sojourner
Tubman, Harriet
Tubular
Tufte, Edward
T□pac Amaru movement
Turing, Alan
Turing test
Turing's law
Turkle, Sherry
Turner, Ted
Turner, Tina
Turntablism
Tuskegee Airmen
Tuskegee experiment
Tutu, Desmond
TV dinner
Twat
Tweak
Twicking
*Twin Peaks*
Twink
Twinkie defense
Twist, the
Twitch speed
*Two Cultures, The*
Two-party system
Tyche
Tyson, Mike

U2
Uinta Mountains
Ukara cloth
Ultimate Thule
*Ulysses*
Umami
Unabomber
Unbundle
UN Declaration of Universal
    Human Rights (1948)
Underworld
Unfriendly
Ungreen
UN High Commissioner for
    Refugees
Unicorns
Uniform resource locator
    (URL)
Uninstall
UN International Children's
    Education Fund
    (UNICEF)
Unionism
United Auto Workers
United Fruit Company
United Indians of All Tribes
United Mine Workers
Universal Service Bus
UNIX
Unleaded
Unmarried mother
Unofficial narratives
UN peace-keeping forces
Unwed pregnancies
Upanishads
Upgrade
Upspeak
Urban legends
Urban renewal
Urban sprawl
Urine test for pregnancy
Usenet
User-friendly

USS Arizona Memorial
Ussher's creation
Uxoricide
Uxorodespotic

Vaccine
*Vagina Monologues*
Vai
Valentine's Day Massacre
Valley Girl
Valspeak
Vampire
Van Buren, Abigail
Vanilla
Vaporware
Vargas Llosa, Mario
Vaticide
V-chip
VCR
Vedas
V-E Day
Vegan
Veganism
Vegetarianism
Velvet revolution
Venice biennial
Ventura, Jessie
Venturi, Robert
Venustaphobia
Verbigerate
Veronica
Versace, Donatella
Versace, Gianni
Vertically challenged
*Vertigo* (1958)
Victimization
Video game rating system
Video games
Videophile
Video store auteurs
Video surveillance
Vidor, King
Viet Nam War Memorial

Villa, Francisco (Pancho)
*Village Voice*
Villa-Lobos, Hector
Vinge, Vernor
Vinyasa yoga
Virago
Virgen de Guadalupe, La
Virgin forest
Virgin of Charity El Cobre
Viridian Greens
Virilio, Paul
Viropause
Virtual
Virtuality
Virtual pets
Virtual reality
Virtual space
Virtual time
Virtual war
Virus (computer)
Vishnu
Visionary
Visual excesses
Visualization
Vixen
Vocational tracks
Vodun
Voice
Voice input
Voicemail
Voiceover
Vonnegut, Kurt
Von Neumann, John
Von Neumann computer
Voodoo
Vortal
Voting Rights Act (1965)
Voucher system
Vox popping
*Voyage of the Damned* (1976)
VPOTUS
Vulnerability
Vulva

Wacko

Waco, Texas

Wages for housework

Wagner Act (1935)

*Waiting for Godot* (1948)

Walbiri

Walcott, Derek

Walesa, Lech

Walker, Alice

Walker, Madame C. J.

Walker, Margaret

Walker, Mort

Walters, John

Wankel engine

Ward, Barbara

Ward, Colin

Ware

Warehouse

War Games Simulation,
      Training and
      Instrumentation
      Command
      (STRICOM)

War on drugs

Warhol, Andy

Warlock

Warren report

Wars of liberation

War-tax resistance

Washington of South America
      (Bolivar)

*Waste Land, The* (1930)

Water-closet

Waters, Muddy

Watts, Alan

Watts race riot (1965)

Watts towers

Weathermen

Weather Underground

Weavers, the

Web of life

Web spider

Web year

Webb, Sidney and Beatrice

Webcam

Weber, Andrew Lloyd

Weber, Max

Webisode

WebTV

Wedlock

Weil, Simone

Weiner, Norbert

Weisman, Fred

Welfare state

*Well of Loneliness, The* (1928)

Wells, Orson

Wells-Barnett, Ida B.

Welty, Eudora

Werewolf

West, Cornel

West, Mae

Western patriarchy

Wetware

Whaling factory ships

Whatever

Wheatley, Phillis

*Wheel of Fortune*

White, Dan

White, E. B.

White, Vanna

White Buffalo Maiden

White-collar crime

White fear

White identity

White Knight

White male supremacy

White man's burden

Whiteness

Whiteness as a social
            construction

Whiteness education

Whiteness studies

White noise

White Owl Woman

White party

White power

White privilege
White rabbit
White racism
White stretch limos
White supremacist
    capitalist patriarchy
White supremacy
White trash
White victimization
Whitney biennial
*Who Wants to be a*
    *Millionaire?*
*Whole Earth Review*
Whore of Babylon
Wiccan rites
Wicked
Wide area network (WAN)
Wigstock
Wilberforce, William
Wild Child of Aveyron
Wilding
Wilkins, Roy
William Morris Agency
Williams, Raymond
Williams, William Carlos
Willis, Paul
Wilson, August
Wilson, Edith
Wimmin
Wimp
Wimple
Window
Wind power
Winfrey, Oprah
Winnage
Winx
Wired
*Wired Magazine*
Wireless
Wire-tapping
Witch
Wizard
Wizard of Menlo Park

*Wizard of Oz, The* (1939)
WNBA
Wobblies
Wolf, Naomi
Wolfe, Thomas
Wollstonecraft, Mary
Womanculture
Womanism
Womanist
Womb
Women's liberation
Women's studies
Women's suffrage
Womyn
Womynist
Wonderbra
Wonder Bread
Wonder Woman
Wonder, Stevie
Woodson, Carter G.
Woodstock
Woodstock nation
Word
Workaholic
Workhouse
Working class
Workplace gender bias
Workplace hierarchy
Work Projects Administration
    (WPA)
Workstation
World Bank
World brain
World social forum
World Trade Center and
    Pentagon Attacks,
    September 11, 2001
World Trade Center Attack of
    1993
World Trade Organization
    (WTO)
World Wide Web (WWW)
Worm

Worm-gear
Worrywart
Wounded Knee
Wozniak, Steve
*Wretched of the Earth, The*
Wright, Frances
Wright, Jay
Wright, Richard
Wright-Edelman, Marian
Writerly texts
Wrongful death
Wrongful life
WTO protests

X
Xanadu
Xanadu computer system
Xanthippe
Xbox
Xenophobic
Xenotransplantation
Xerography
Xerox parc
*X-Files*
*X-Men*

Yacht people
Yada yada yada
Yahoo
Yahoo (web directory)
Yakuza
Yam
Yamanaka, Lois-Ann
Yashmak
Yeager, Chuck
Year 2000 problem (Y2K)
Yellow journalism
Yellow kid
Yellow ribbon (war)
"Yellow Submarine"
Yo
Yom Kippur war
Yoruba

Young, Andrew Jackson
Young, Chic
Yo-yo
Yo-yo mode
Yule
Yuppie
Yuppie flu

Zamboni
Zangwell, Israel
Zap
Zap Comix
Zapatistas
Zappa, Frank
Zapping
Zapruder film
Zarf
Zeitgeist
*Zelig* (1983)
*Zena*
Zeno's law
Zeppelin
Zero option
Zero tolerance
Zine
Zinn, Howard
Zion
Zizith
Zöetrope
ZoidZone
Zombie
Zone
Zonk out
Zoom shot
Zoonosis
Zoophobia
Zoot suit
Zoot-suit riot (1942)
Zori
Zouk
Zucchetto
Zulu time
Zworykin, Vladimir

# BIBLIOGRAPHY

Allman, P., "Gramsci, Freire and Illich: Their Contributions to Education for Socialism." In Tom Lovett, ed., *Radical Approaches to Adult Education.* London: Routledge, 1988.

Apple, M. W. *Educating the "Right" Way: Markets, Standards, God, and Inequality.* New York: Routledge Falmer, 2001.

―――. *Official Knowledge: Democratic Education in a Conservative Age.* New York: Routledge, 2000.

―――. *Power, Meaning, and Identity: Essays in Critical Educational Studies.* New York: P. Lang, 1999.

―――. *Cultural Politics and Education.* Philadelphia: Open University Press, 1996.

―――. *Education and Power.* New York: Routledge, 1995.

―――. *Teachers and Texts: A Political Economy of Class and Gender Relations in Education.* New York: Routledge & Kegan Paul, 1985.

―――. *Cultural and Economic Reproduction in Education: Essays on Class, Ideology, and the State.* London and Boston: Routledge & Kegan Paul, 1982.

―――. *Ideology and Curriculum.* Boston: Routledge & Kegan Paul, 1979.

Apple, M. W., and J. A. Beane. *Democratic Schools.* Alexandria, VA.: Association for Supervision and Curriculum Development, 1995.

Aronowitz, Stanley, and Henry A. Giroux. *Postmodern Education: Politics, Culture, and Social Criticism.* Minneapolis: University of Minnesota Press, 1991.

Barton, L., R. Meighan, et al. *Schooling, Ideology, and the Curriculum.* London: Falmer, 1980.

Gregory Bateson. *Mind and Nature: A Necessary Unity.* New York: Bantam Books, 1980.

Bennett, William J. *First Lessons: A Report on Elementary Education in America.* Washington, D.C.: U.S. Dept. of Education, U.S. G.P.O., 1986.

―――. *Our Children and Our Country: Improving America's Schools and Affirming the Common Culture.* New York: Simon and Schuster, 1988.

Bennett, William J., and Educational Resources Information Center (U.S.). *James Madison High School: A Curriculum for American Students.* Washington, D.C.: Dept. of Education, Educational Resources Information Center, 1987.

Bennett, William J., and the United States Department of Education. *American Education: Making it Work: A Report to the President and the American People.* Washington, D.C.: U.S. Dept. of Education, 1988.

Bennett, William J., and the United States Department of Education. Office of the Secretary. *Address by William J. Bennett, United States Secretary of Education: Education for Democracy.* Washington, D.C.: U.S. Dept. of Education, 1986.

————. *Address by William J. Bennett, United States Secretary of Education: Harvard University, Cambridge, Massachusetts.* Washington, D.C.: U.S. Dept. of Education, 1986.

Bennett, William J. *A Strategy for Transforming America's Culture, Heritage Lectures, 489.* Washington, D.C.: The Heritage Foundation, 1994.

————. *First Lessons: A Report on Elementary Education in America.* Washington, D.C.: U.S. Dept. of Education, 1986.

Bennett, William J., and Hudson Institute. *Proposal: The Modern Red Schoolhouse.* Indianapolis: Hudson Institute, 1992.

Bennett, William J., and the United States Department of Education. *American Education: Making It Work. A Report to the President and the American People.* Washington, D.C.: U.S. Dept. of Education, 1988.

Bennett, William J., Chester E. Finn, and John T. E. Cribb. *The Educated Child: A Parent's Guide from Preschool through Eighth Grade.* New York: Free Press, 1999.

Bennett, William J., and Dana B. Ciccone. *What Works: William J. Bennett's Research About Teaching and Learning.* Wooster, Ohio: Wooster Book Co., 1996.

Bennett, William J. *The Book of Virtues: A Treasury of Great Moral Stories.* New York: Simon & Schuster, 1993.

————. *The De-Valuing of America: The Fight for Our Culture and Our Children.* New York: Summit Books, 1992.

————. *Our Children and Our Country: Improving America's Schools and Affirming the Common Culture.* New York: Simon and Schuster, 1988.

Berliner, David, and Bruce Biddle, *The Manufactured Crisis: Myths, Fraud, and the Attack on America's Public Schools.* Reading, MA: Addison-Wesley 1995.

Bestor, Arthur E. Jr., "Life Adjustment in Education: A Critique," *American Association of University Professors Bulletin*, 38 (1952): 413-441.

————. *Educational Wastelands: The Retreat from Learning in Our Public Schools* . Urbana, Ill.: University of Illinois Press, 1953.

Bloom, Allan. *The Closing of the American Mind.* New York: Simon and Schuster, 1987.

Boggs, C. *Gramsci's Marxism.* London: Pluto Press, 1976.

Buras, Kristin L., "Questioning Core Assumptions: A Critical Reading of and Response to E. D. Hirsch's *The Schools We Need and Why We Don't Have Them,*" *Harvard Educational Review*, 69;1 (Spring 1999): 67–93.

Callahan, Raymond C. *Education and the Cult of Efficiency.* Chicago: University of Chicago Press, 1962.

Carlson, Dennis, and Michael W. Apple. *Power, Knowledge, Pedagogy: the Meaning of Democratic Education in Unsettling Times.* Boulder, Colo, Westview Press, 1998.

Carnoy, M. *Faded Dreams: The Politics and Economics of Race in America.* Cambridge UK: Cambridge University Press, 1994.

Carnoy, M., and H. M. Levin. *Schooling and Work in the Democratic State.* Stanford, Calif.: Stanford University Press, 1985.

Carnoy, M. *Schooling in a Corporate Society: The Political Economy of Education in America.* New York: McKay, 1975.

Carnoy, Martin, 1974. *Education as Cultural Imperialism.* New York: David McKay Company.

Collins, Randall. *The Credential Society.* New York: Academic Press, 1971.

Core Knowledge Foundation. *Core Knowledge Sequence (Revised 1995): Content Guide for Grades K-6.* Charlottesville, Virginia: Core Knowledge Foundation, 1995.

Cuban, Larry. *How Teachers Taught: Constancy and Change in American Classrooms, 1890-1990.* New York: Teachers College Press, 1993.

Dewey, John. "My Pedagogic Creed," *Journal of the National Education Association*, Vol. 18, No. 9, pp. 291–295, December, 1929.

———. *Democracy and Education.* New York: The Free Press, 1944.

———. *The School and Society; and the Child and the Curriculum* (New York: Dover Books, 2001).

Dykhuizen, George. *The Life and Mind of John Dewey* (Carbondale: University of Southern Illinois Press, 1973).

Educational Resources Information Center (U.S.). *Conversations on Excellence in Education. A Regional Leadership Conference, Rosemont, Pennsylvania, May 11, 1985.* Washington, D.C.: U.S. Dept. of Education Office of Educational Research and Improvement Educational Resources Information Center, 1985.

Eisner, Elliot W. *The Educational Imagination: On the Design and Evaluation of School Programs* (3rd edition). New York: Macmillan, 1994.

———. *The Educational Imagination: On the Design and_Evaluation of School Programs,* 2nd edn. New York: MacMillan, 1985.

Entwistle, H. *Antonio Gramsci: Conservative Schooling for Radical Politics.* London: Routledge, 1979.

Feinberg, Walter, "Educational Manifestoes and the New Fundamentalism," *Educational Researcher*, 26;8: 27–35.

Freire, Paulo. *Cultural Action for Freedom.* Cambridge: Harvard Educational Review Monographs, 1970.

————. *Education for Critical Consciousness.* New York: Seabury Press, 1973.

————. *Pedagogy of the Oppressed.* New York: Herder & Herder, 1970.

Fuller, Harry J. "The Emperor's New Clothes, or prius dementat," *The Scientific Monthly,* 72(1951): 32–41.

Gallup Organization, "31st Annual Phi Delta Kappa/Gallup Poll of the Public's Attitudes Toward the Public Schools," *Phi Delta Kappan.* 81(1999): 41–56.

————. "24th Annual Phi Delta Kappa/Gallup Poll of the Public's Attitudes Toward the Public Schools," *Phi Delta Kappan.* 74(1992): 41–53.

————. "18th Annual Phi Delta Kappa/Gallup Poll of the Public's Attitudes Toward the Public Schools," *Phi Delta Kappan.* 68(1986): 43–59.

Gardner, Howard, "Toward Good Thinking On Essential Questions," *New York Times*, September 11, 1999:A15, A17.

Giddens, A. *Sociology.* 3rd ed. Cambridge: Polity Press, 1997.

Giroux, Henry. *The Abandoned Generation: Democracy Beyond the Culture of Fear.* New York: Palgrave, 2003.

————. *Stealing Innocence: Youth, Corporate Power, and the Politics of Culture.* New York: St. Martin's Press, 2000.

————. *Pedagogy and the Politics of Hope: Theory, Culture, and Schooling: A Critical Reader, The Edge, Critical Studies in Educational Theory.* Boulder, CO: Westview Press, 1997.

————. *Counternarratives: Cultural Studies and Critical Pedagogies in Postmodern Spaces.* New York: Routledge, 1996.

————. *Disturbing Pleasures: Learning Popular Culture.* New York: Routledge, 1994.

————. *Living Dangerously: Multiculturalism and the Politics of Difference.* New York: P. Lang, 1993.

————. *Border Crossings: Cultural Workers and the Politics of Education.* New York; London: Routledge, 1992.

————. *Postmodernism, Feminism, and Cultural Politics: Redrawing Educational Boundaries.* Albany: State University of New York Press, 1991.

————. *Teachers as Intellectuals: Toward a Critical Pedagogy of Learning.* Granby, MA: Bergin & Garvey Publishers, Inc., 1988.

————. *Ideology, Culture, and the Process of Schooling.* Philadelphia: Temple University Press, 1981.

————. *Critical Pedagogy, the State, and Cultural Struggle, Teacher Empowerment and School Reform.* Albany: State University of New York Press, 1989.

Giroux, Henry A., and Peter McLaren. *Between Borders: Pedagogy and the Politics of Cultural Studies.* New York; London: Routledge, 1994.

Giroux, Henry A., and Patrick Shannon. *Education and Cultural Studies: Toward a Performative Practice.* New York: Routledge, 1997.

Gitlin, Todd. *The Whole World is Watching: Mass Media in the Making and Unmaking of the New Left.* Berkeley, CA: University of California Press, 1980.

———. *The Twilight of Common Dreams: Why America Is Wracked by Culture Wars.* New York: Henry Holt and Company, 1995.

Graff, Gerald. *Beyond the Culture Wars: How Teaching the Conflicts Can Revitalize American Education.* New York: W. W. Norton, 1992.

Gramsci, A. *Selections from the Prison Notebooks.* London: Lawrence and Wishart, 1971.

———. *Selections From The Prison Notebooks of Antonio Gramsci,* ed. Q. Hoare and G. Nowell-Smith. New York: International Publishers, 1971.

Greene, Maxine. *Teacher as Stranger.* Belmont, CA: Wadsworth, 1973.

———. Review of Cultural Literacy, by E. D. Hirsch, Jr., *Teachers College Record* 90, No. 1, (Fall, 1988) pp. 149–155.

Grumet, Madeline R., *"The Curriculum: What Are the Basics and Why Are We Teaching Them?"* In Joe L. Kinchloe and Shirley R. Steinberg, eds. *Thirteen Questions: Reframing Education's Conversation.* 2d ed. New York: Peter Lang, 1995: 15–21.

Habermäs, Jurgen. *Legitimation Crisis.* Boston: Beacon Press, 1973.

Hadingham, Evan. *Ancient Chinese Explorers* Nova Online at: http://www.pbs.org/wgbh/nova/sultan/explorers.html.

Hertzberg, Hazel Whitman, "Review of *Cultural Literacy: What Every American Needs to Know,*" *Teachers College Record* 90, No. 1(Fall 1988): 145–148.

Henry, Jules. *On Education.* New York: Vintage Books, 1972.

Hirsch, E. D., "Finding the Answers in Drills and Rigor," *New York Times,* September 11, 1999: A15, A17.

———. *Cultural Literacy: What Every American Needs to Know.* New York: Vintage Books, 1988.

———. *Cultural Literacy: What Every American Needs to Know.* Boston: Houghton Mifflin, 1987.

———. *What Your Fourth Grader Needs to Know: Fundamentals of a Good Fourth-Grade Education.* New York, Doubleday 1992.

———. *What Your Fifth Grader Needs to Know: Fundamentals of a Good Fifth-Grade Education.* New York, Doubleday, 1993.

———. *What Your Sixth Grader Needs to Know: Fundamentals of a Good Sixth-Grade Education.* 1st ed., The Core Knowledge Series; Bk. 6. New York: Doubleday, 1993.

———. *The Schools We Need and Why We Don't Have Them.* 1st ed. New York: Doubleday, 1996.

————. *What Your Kindergartner Needs to Know: Preparing Your Child for a Lifetime of Learning.* 1st ed., The Core Knowledge Series. New York: Doubleday, 1996.

————. *What Your First Grader Needs to Know: Fundamentals of a Good First-Grade Education.* Rev. ed. The Core Knowledge Series. New York: Doubleday, 1997.

————. "Response to Professor Feinberg," *Educational Researcher*, March 1998: 38–39.

————. *What Your Third Grader Needs to Know: Fundamentals of a Good Third-Grade Education.* Rev. ed, The Core Knowledge Series. New York: Doubleday, 2001.

Hirsch, E. D., Joseph F. Kett, and James S. Trefil. *The Dictionary of Cultural Literacy.* Boston: Houghton Mifflin, 1988.

————. *The Dictionary of Cultural Literacy.* 2nd ed. Boston: Houghton Mifflin, 1993.

Hirsch, E. D., and John Holdren. *What Your Second Grader Needs to Know: Fundamentals of a Good Second-Grade Education.* Rev. ed, The Core Knowledge Series. New York: Doubleday, 1998.

Hochschild, Adam. *King Leopold's Ghost—A Story of Greed, Terror and Heroism in Colonial Africa.* New York: Macmillan, 1998.

Kanpol, B., and P. McLaren. *Critical Multiculturalism: Uncommon Voices in a Common Struggle.* Westport, CT: Bergin & Garvey, 1995.

Kelly, Gail P., and Phillip Altbach. *Education and Colonialism.* New York: Longman, 1978.

Kincheloe, Joe L. *White Reign: Deploying Whiteness in America.* New York: St. Martin's Press, 1998.

Kincheloe, Joe L., and Shirley R. Steinberg. *Changing Multiculturalism.* Buckingham and Philadelphia: Open University Press, 1997.

————. *Thirteen Questions: Reframing Education's Conversation.* New York, Peter Lang, 1995.

————. *Changing Multiculturalism.* Buckingham, U.K.; Philadelphia: Open University Press, 1997.

Kliebard, Herbert M. *Forging the American Curriculum: Essays in Curriculum History and Theory.* New York: Routledge, 1992.

————. *The Struggle for the American Curriculum, 1893-1958.* 2nd ed. New York: Routledge, 1995.

Kozol, Jonathan. *On Being a Teacher.* New York: Continuum, 1981.

Leistyna, P., A. Woodrum, et al. *Breaking Free: The Transformative Power of Critical Pedagogy.* Cambridge, MA: Harvard Educational Review, 1996.

Lynd, Albert. *Quackery in the Public Schools.* Boston: Little Brown, 1953.

Macedo, Donaldo P. *Literacies of Power: What Americans Are Not Allowed to Know* (Boulder, CO: Westview Press, 1996).

————. "A Dialogue: Culture, Language and Race (Interview with Paulo Freire), *Harvard Educational Review* 3 (Fall 1995), pp. 377–403.

McLaren, Peter. *Life in Schools: An Introduction to Critical Pedagogy in the Foundations of Education.* New York, Longman, 1989.

————. *Critical Pedagogy and Predatory Culture: Oppositional Politics in a Postmodern Era.* New York: Routledge, 1995.

————. *Revolutionary Multiculturalism: Pedagogies of Dissent for the New Millennium.* Boulder, CO: Westview Press, 1997.

————. *Life in schools: An Introduction to Critical Pedagogy in the Foundations of Education.* 3d Ed. New York: Longman, 1998.

————. *Schooling as a Ritual Performance: Toward a Political Economy of Educational Symbols and Gestures.* Lanham, MD: Rowman & Littlefield, 1999.

Meyer, J. W. "The effects of educational organizations." In Marshall Meyer & Associates, eds., *Environments and Organizations.* San Francisco: Jossey-Bass, 1997: 78–109.

National Commission on Excellence in Education. *A Nation at Risk: The Imperative for Educational Reform.* Washington, D.C.: Government Printing Office, 1983.

O'Donnell, James J. *Avatars of the Word: From Papyrus to Cyberspace.* Cambridge: Harvard University Press, 1998.

Ognibene, Richard. "Social Foundations and School Reform Networks: The Case of E. D. Hirsch," *Educational Foundations*, Vol. 12, #4, Fall 1998: 5-27.

Ovando, C. J., and P. McLaren. *The Politics of Multiculturalism and Bilingual Education: Students and Teachers Caught in the Cross Fire.* Boston: McGraw-Hill, 2000.

Persell, Caroline Hodge, Sophia Catsambis, and Peter Cookson, Jr. "Family Background, School Type, and College Attendence: A Cojoint System of Cultural Capital Transmission," *Journal of Research on Adolescence*, 2 (1992): 1–23.

Petrovic, John. "Dewey Is a Philistine and Other Grave Misreadings," *Oxford Review of Education*, 24(4) (1998): 513–520.

Presley, Michael, "We Still Know Little About the Schools that E. D. Hirsch Believes We Need," *Issues in Education*, 3;1 (1997): 135–151.

Ravitch, Diane. *Left Back: A Century of Failed School Reforms.* New York: Simon and Schuster, 2000.

Schuster, Edgar, "In Pursuit of Cultural Literacy," *Phi Delta Kappan*, 70 (1989): 539–542.

Simonson, Rick, and Scott Walker, eds. *The Graywolf Annual Five: Multicultural Literacy.* Saint Paul, MN: Graywolf Press, 1988.

Smith, Mortimor B. *And Madly Teach.* Chicago: Henry Regnery, 1949.

Smith, Linda Tuhuwai. *Decolonizing Methodologies: Research and Indigenous Peoples.* London: Zed Books, 1999.

Spring, Joel H. *Deculturalization and the Struggle for Equality: A Brief History of the Education of Dominated Cultures in the United States.* Boston, McGraw-Hill, 2001.

Stedman, Lawrence. "The Achievement Crisis is Real: A Review of the Manufactured Crisis," *Education Policy Analysis Archives*, 4:1 (January 23, 1996). Available online at: http://epaa.asu.edu/epaa/v4n1.html.

Steinberg, Shirley R. *Multi/intercultural Conversations: A Reader.* New York: Peter Lang, 2001.

Tanner, L. N. *Dewey's Laboratory School: Lessons for Today.* New York: Teachers College Press, 1997.

Treifel, James, Joseph F. Kett, and E. D. Hirsch, Jr., editors. *The New Dictionary of Cultural Literacy: What Every American Needs to* Know. Boston: Houghton Mifflin Co., 2002.

United States Department of Education. *A Nation at Risk: The Imperative of Educational Reform.* Washington, D. C.: Government Printing Office, 1983.

Whitehead, Alfred North. *The Aims of Education and Other Essays.* New York: The Free Press, 1957.

Willinsky, John. *Learning to Divide the World: Education at Empire's End.* Minneapolis, MN: University of Minnesota Press, 1998.

Willis, P. E. *Learning to Labor: How Working Class Kids Get Working Class Jobs.* New York, Columbia University Press, 1981.

Wirth, A. G. *John Dewey as Educator: His Design for Work in Education (1894-1904).* Lanham, MD: University Press of America, 1989.

# INDEX